Dedication

I dedicate this book to my wife Lisa who has taught me more than anyone else and supported me at every turn. I love you so much. I also dedicate this book to my three children Charissa, Justin and Jesse and their families. I am blessed beyond measure to have the greatest kids in the world!

Acknowledgements

This book is not possible without the Zechariah 4 family. You pulled this book out of me! Thank you for all of your love, prayers, and support.

Thank you Chris Link for doing all the hard work of putting this book together. You were the one that gave me the push I needed to get it done! Thank you Anthony Garcia for the amazing cover picture, it captures the whole book!

Thank you Jesus for touching me so many years ago and giving me true abundant life and an incredible relationship that I will enjoy for all eternity!

THE CEASELESS FLOW OF OIL

by Tim Lighthall

Introduction

It was a time of government takeovers and economic crisis. The leaders of the nation were more corrupt that anyone before or after. Great judgment was upon the nation. The king had made alliances with other evil nations that heaped their sin into the mix as well. It was one of the darkest times tiny Israel had ever faced. Could they survive such an onslaught of rebellion against the morals and beliefs of a nation as well as against God Himself? Would God's judgment wipe out men and women, young and old?

Let's pick up the story in 1 Kings 17. We read the story of how Ahab and Jezebel had turned a nation so far away from God, that God had to put His plan of restoration and redemption into motion. That same pattern of restoration is applicable today in our nation and any other nation needing to be restored back to its God called destiny! No nation is beyond the love and mercy of God. If the nation would just humble themselves and turn back to their God, seeking His face, He would bring restoration and healing to the people, the economy, the government, the family, the education system, the culture, and every area of society. Interestingly enough, the plan involved a ceaseless flow of provision and prosperity as well as a ceaseless flow of His presence and power!

God often brings restoration to a nation by first raising up men and/or women of God in the midst of the crisis. Elijah was called and sent to the Brook Cherith (meaning covenant) to drink of that brook until the water ran out because there was no rain and would not be any rain for three years. Water was the foundation of that agricultural nation, without it, the plants would die as would the animals that fed on the plants as would the people who fed on the meat and plants. It was truly an economic crisis at least, a life and death crisis at most. So the Lord sends Elijah to drink of the truths of His covenant. He drank up the truths of the covenant until there was no more to drink. Elijah had to be filled to the full of his understanding of how God's Kingdom works through the promises made to Abraham, Isaac, and Jacob. Elijah also was fed by the ravens. The word raven describes the look of the bird, the look of the setting of the sun bringing darkness over the land. It was truly a time of the sun setting over Israel, the nation was entering a night season in order to see the deliverance of the Lord. The Brook Cherith also flowed into the Jordan, meaning descent, the people were descending into a time of going through the valley. Yet God knew exactly what He was doing, as He does nothing outside of His own covenant He makes with His people. God is raising up men and women of God in this day and teaching them about covenant, about how the promises of God are yes and amen in Jesus. He is revealing again how His grace is sufficient and how trust in Him can restore a nation. The church must learn that nations are blessed depending upon the church being salt and light to that nation or cursed by allowing that nation to plummet into darkness due to their complacency and being lukewarm.

Elijah stayed at the brook for quite a while but after the river dried up, after he had received all the meat and water (the truths concerning God's covenant plans for restoration), the Lord sent him to a widow of Zarephath (meaning place of refinement) which belongs to Zidon (the place of catching fish, the place of ministry, the place where she was dying instead of fulfilling her God-given destiny). The widow, representing the church who has lost her husband or her spiritual leaders (who also had become complacent and lacked knowledge of the covenant and had left their congregations hungry, miserable, and ready to leave church and die spiritually) was there gathering her resources for one more meal for her and her son (the next generation of believers that were also affected and dying). It was at that point she met Elijah. He asks her for a drink and a meal, and she confesses she has only a little meal of flour (representing the Word of God), a little oil (representing the Holy Spirit and the anointing or power of God), and two sticks (representing her salvation, the cross of Jesus). She said she was going to make one last meal with what she had to work with (represents the works the church has fallen into because of their lack of covenant understanding of grace), but she knew in the end it would result in death. A little word, a little anointing, but no grace covenant will kill the church every time.

Elijah, overflowing at this point with the truth of covenant, tells her that if she makes the meal and gives it to him, she would experience a ceaseless flow of provision and later, when the rains came, she would experience a ceaseless flow of prosperity. She just had to come into agreement with the leader sent by God. Today, also, the Lord desires to wake up the widowed saints! She did, and Elijah spent time with her pouring into her all he had learned about covenant, all the while she was miraculously provided for as was Elijah. The ceaseless flow is available today to all who understand covenant and partner with leaders who pour into them God's promises.

The ceaseless flow of oil does not guarantee that nothing bad will ever happen to us, but it does guarantee that God will make a way according to His covenant to minister to us in our times of crisis. The widow's son dies during this visitation from Elijah and Elijah lays on the boy three times and the boy is raised from the dead. Then she makes a powerful declaration, "Now I know that you are a man of God and that the Word of the Lord in your mouth is true." She had heard the truth about covenant, she had seen the miraculous ceaseless flow of provision, but this miracle made a true believer out of her. She replies that all that he had been teaching her had been confirmed, it was true, and that he truly is a man of God. Bottom line, she was the first fruits of the restoration and redemption. Do we want that for our nation? Then it starts with the church!

This pattern is the same pattern needed to restore a nation. God raises up leaders, teaches those leaders about His ways, truths, and paths, about His covenant and all His promises and how to access them, then He sends those leaders to a hungry remnant who see the word confirmed with manifestations. I believe the church is at the point of manifestation. We have leaders who finally get it, the truth of the covenant of grace and favor, the covenant of the Good News of Jesus Christ, the Gospel of the Kingdom of God and has been sharing these truths with signs confirming what they teach. As the church gets in order, Elijah and the widow will be prepared to face the people of a nation who are under the deception of baal worship (1 Kings 18), and God will demonstrate to them that He is God by sending fire from heaven if necessary. Then the leadership will be granted power and authority to call in new governmental leaders (1 Kings 19) and the nation will experience revival and restoration!!!

This powerful story is not the only passage about a ceaseless flow. 2 Kings 4 tells the story of Elisha telling the widow to go get empty vessels and begin pouring oil into them and that the oil would not run out until they stopped pouring into empty vessels! This reveals God's plan as to how to experience a ceaseless flow of transformed lives. We are to take the little oil He has given us, and we are to go to the empty vessels around us in our neighborhoods, communities, regions and nations and begin to minister to them, pouring out the little anointing we have, and the anointing will multiply and never run out unless we quit seeking more empty vessels. The story also represents prosperity, as oil was a very important marketplace commodity. As the widow gave, it was given back to her pressed down, shaken together, and running over. Prosperity, again, was a ceaseless flow. We are in desperate need of a ceaseless flow of His presence, power, and peace (shalom, prosperity and wholeness in every area of life).

Ezekiel 47 describes a flow of water that began as a trickle coming out of the Holy of Holies (see the chapter on the priestly anointing to see how to get the trickle started) and began to flow and even rise until it got to the place where it healed all the fish (lost people) in the sea! The further the flow got away from the church and toward the lost, the stronger the flow became! This theme of a ceaseless flow is a beautiful description of God's love and His mercies which are flowing new every day, and His desire to bless us so we can be a blessing to others. Days of hit and miss miracles need to end, we need to move into the days of a ceaseless flow that many have longed for, prayed for, and expected. You can follow God's pattern of the ceaseless flow and experience its manifestation! You can be transformed, your family can be transformed, your church, your community, and even your nation can experience reformation as we understand the truths about God's ceaseless flow. His ceaseless flow of oil represents all the that the Holy Spirit is and does. We can have a ceaseless flow of anointing, of salvations and transformed lives, of revelation, of wisdom, of miracles, of finances, of holiness, of all the Holy Spirit is, and most importantly, a ceaseless flow of intimacy with Jesus!!

There is another story of a ceaseless flow, and it will be the foundation for the rest of this book. It is found in Zechariah 4. My prayer is that as you read this, the ceaseless flow of oil will begin flowing and increasing and abounding in your life!!

Table of Contents

Chapter 1: The Ceaseless Flow of Oil!

I received a phone call from a woman in Washington state telling me her sister was in the hospital in Naples, Florida, about a half an hour from our ministry location. She told me that her sister was very sick and so she searched online for ministries in our area that believed in healing. She found our ministry, called, and I told her that yes, we believed in praying for the sick, so she asked if we would please go pray for her sister. Of course, we said we would, and a few days later we put a team of eight together and hopped in the vehicle to go to Naples. Others stayed behind to pray. We just began to receive His presence and power as we travelled down the interstate. By the time we got to the hospital, we were so full of the presence and power of God that we could hardly get out of the SUV! We knew that the sickness we were about to confront did not have a chance! We all walked up to the hospital room and they let us all in the room (a miracle in itself!). As we walked in the hospital, the presence of God, a ceaseless flow of Him, came with us! We went into the room, made introductions (after the atheist nurse ran out of the room unable to stay in the presence) and then we began to pray for this wonderful lady named Teresa. She was covered up by a blanket so we could not see her distended stomach nor did we know that 19 doctors had been working with her and could not come to a diagnosis let alone a cure. It was later realized she was in lupus crisis amidst so many other physical issues. As we shared with her about God's love, about the Holy Spirit, and about healing, we then simply anointed her with oil, did some simple deliverance acts, released healing and then we left the hospital. She told us later (we did not know what happened to her for a few months) that when we prayed she felt like rocket power hit her body and her stomach instantly "deflated" and she was healed! She was out of the hospital in just a few days and all of her bloodwork was completely normal after many years of physical suffering and pain. No one survives a lupus crisis but she did! The Holy Spirit had shown up and instantly healed her miraculously! But He was not done! We need the flow to start but never to stop. Since that day she has shared that testimony of healing many times over, seen many healed, saved, and set free! She is one of the most on fire lovers of Jesus I know. The Spirit wants to touch your life and never stop flowing!!! How can all of us experience this ceaseless flow of oil?

Zechariah 4 chronicles the vision God gave the prophet about a ceaseless flow of oil to the candlestick. If we can grasp what this vision means, we, too, can see that ceaseless flow of oil restored back to the Kingdom! Let's look at the context and contents of this chapter in the Amplified translation.

First, let's look at the context of this passage. Chapter three is the beautiful picture of salvation, where satan argues for Joshua's (the High Priest) soul. The Lord rebukes the enemy and changes Joshua's filthy rags for clean. It is a wonderful picture of salvation. To add to the wonder of the passage, in verse nine it talks about the baptism of the Spirit, where the seven eyes of the Spirit are set before or given to Joshua. This is a picture of the church today. We have been gloriously saved and wonderfully baptized in the Spirit, yet we do not see the ceaseless flow of oil. It is in this context that Zechariah sees the vision in chapter 4.

"AND THE angel who talked with me came again and awakened me, like a man who is wakened out of his sleep. And said to me, What do you see? I said, I see, and behold, a lampstand all of gold, with its bowl [for oil] on the top of it and its seven lamps on it, and [there are] seven pipes to each of the seven lamps which are upon the top of it. And there are two olive trees by it, one upon the right side of the bowl and the other upon the left side of it [feeding it continuously with oil]." (Zechariah 4:1-3)

The first verse is extremely important. The body of Christ has been asleep. We desperately need an awakening. We have lived off of half the inheritance for too long (The baptism of the Spirit as represented by the candlestick in the tabernacle is only half way to the Holy of Holies. We have fallen short of the goal! For all have sinned and fallen short of the *glory* of God. The glory of God is the goal! True salvation should put people on the journey toward the glory of God! We became content in the midst of that journey by seeking His hand rather than with His face! We must move on to the intimacy of the Holy of Holies!). God gives Zechariah a wake up call saying that there is more! There is a ceaseless flow of oil! This should wake us up! For those who do believe it, they will wake up, knowing that an unprecedented move of God is available!

The vision Zechariah saw was that of a candlestick (representing the Holy Spirit), but it had seven pipes on the sides of the candlestick and a continuous flow of oil was flowing through the pipes. The pipes were coming from olive trees, one on each side of the candlestick. The flow was to be so great that there was a need for pipes to handle the great flow. We understand the Amplified translation's adding to the text that it was feeding continuously because it was not a single olive that was providing the flow, it was the whole tree. There was a never-ending supply. Therefore it should be seen, as the Amplified translation does, that there was a continuous flow or feeding of the oil from the tree through the pipeline to the candlestick. We must understand what the two olive trees represent. If we can get the understanding of this, we, too, can have a continual or ceaseless flow of the oil of the Holy Spirit in our lives and in our churches!

Before we get to what the two olive trees represent, let's follow the passage.

"So I asked the angel who talked with me, What are these, my lord? Then the angel who talked with me answered me, Do you not know what these are? And I said, No, my lord. Then he said to me,

3

This [addition of the bowl to the candlestick, causing it to yield a ceaseless supply of oil from the olive trees] is the word of the Lord to Zerubbabel, saying, Not by might, nor by power, but by My Spirit [of Whom the oil is a symbol], says the Lord of hosts." (Zechariah 4:4-6)

Zechariah had to be about beside himself when he saw the vision! We should be beside ourselves longing to get the understanding of this vision for today! A ceaseless flow of the manifestations of the Holy Spirit! WOW! What will we not do to see this passage come true in our day! So Zechariah urgently asked the angel of the Lord what the vision meant. The angel gave the obvious answer, that the candlestick represented the Holy Spirit. We, as a Body of Christ, have substituted programs, works, and gimmicks for the Holy Spirit. We have tried imitating other churches that are successful, we have tried worldly means, we have tried everything under the sun except the ceaseless flow of oil. When the ceaseless flow breaks out, there will never be another need for a gimmick nor for our own strength and power. Everything will be done by the power of the Holy Spirit. It has been said that if the Holy Spirit was taken out of most churches, 95% of what they do would continue. When this outpouring occurs, the world will stand up and take notice. Adrian Rogers rightly said, "We have no right to be believed, as long as we can be explained." When the ceaseless flow is loosed, the church and the world will begin to see what no eye has seen nor ear has heard nor minds have imagined. We will finally see the "greater works" that Jesus talked about, the "rivers of living water" flowing out of our innermost being, and we will see them on a regular basis!

The Lord continues speaking to Zechariah through the angel of the Lord saying:

"For who are you, O great mountain [of human obstacles]? Before Zerubbabel [who with Joshua had led the return of the exiles from Babylon and was undertaking the rebuilding of the temple, before him] you shall become a plain [a mere molehill]! And he shall bring forth the finishing gable stone [of the new temple] with loud

—

4

shoutings of the people, crying, 'Grace, grace to it!'" *(Zechariah 4:7)*

This is great news! This tells us that according to Zechariah's end time vision there is coming a day that the mountains of the world, the flesh, and the demonic strongholds are going to be wiped out! After they are wiped out the top stone or the last piece of the building of the spiritual house that God has been building since day one will be put on! It will not be done because of us it will be done in spite of us and the generation that understands this vision and lives it will know that they know it is only by God's grace that it happened. It will be so obvious it is done for us that we will **shout** "Grace, grace" to it! There is coming a day that the ceaseless flow will start flowing but it will not flow until there is a great repentance in the Body of Christ. The heights of revival are dependent on the depths of repentance. The depths of repentance are dependent upon the heights of hunger. So for the remnant in the church that is not lukewarm but is desperately asking, seeking, and knocking, the Lord Himself will bring down the sin that so easily entangles us and the mountain of sin and distraction and religion will become a plain! Jesus gave a parable about the Kingdom in Matthew 13:41-43 that said that He would send angels to gather every obstacle to righteousness and would completely remove it! The Lord will make sure these obstacles to a spotless bride are removed. It is also important that we understand that the mountain will come down before Zerubbabel. It will only happen when divine order is established. This will be explained more later, but without the government of God in place in the Body of Christ, no mountains will ever be made into plains. Ephesians 4:13 says that the government of the church (represented here by Zerubbabel, the governor) will lead to a people being perfected or matured where sin has been dealt with in their lives. Again, more will be said about this later.

Next, the Lord says unto Zechariah:

"Moreover, the word of the Lord came to me, saying, 'The hands of Zerubbabel have laid the foundations of this house; his hands shall also finish it. Then you shall know (recognize and understand) that

the Lord of hosts has sent me [His messenger] to you. Who [with reason] despises the day of small things? For these seven shall rejoice when they see the plummet in the hand of Zerubbabel. [These seven] are the eyes of the Lord which run to and fro throughout the whole earth.'" (Zechariah 4:8-10)

We again see the importance of the government of God. We see here that the Lord says that His government (again represented by Zerubbabel the governor and represented by a hand symbolizing the five-fold leadership of the church found in Ephesians 4:11) laid the foundation of the spiritual house made of living stones which Christ Jesus is the Chief Cornerstone (see Isaiah 9:6, 1 Peter 2:4-6). We also know that God's government will bring this unceasing flow into existence (will finish it, meaning that it will be an end times event). Therefore, we are already seeing in this passage the importance of understanding God's government and divine order in the church. When we see this happen; we will know it is of the Lord. It will start small as it will be led by a remnant, but we are not to despise small beginnings. It is small because the road is narrow that leads to life, there are few that find it. According to 1 Corinthians 2:6-7 and 3:1-3 Paul says that there are two kinds of Christians. One kind is a carnal kind that is still fleshly and sipping their milk. The other kind of Christian is the one that is mature and yearns for and comes to understand even the mysteries of God. These are the hungry. These are the ones that give God no rest until Jerusalem becomes a praise in the earth. These are the ones that are hearing the Lord knocking and are opening the door after they realized how poor, blind and naked they were. These are the ones that are like the persistent widow crying out to God for revival. These are the ones that are tired of church and Christianity as usual. They are the ones stopping at nothing to get the "more"! This is the remnant Isaiah talks about that will sow deep and bear much fruit upward after too long of the church flying by the seat of its pants (Isaiah 19:29-31). These are the people that are not content with the inner court, they long for the Holy of Holies! This small group of people have begun to find one another and have gotten into a Psalm 133 type unity and are crying out until the oil is loosed! It may start small but it will eventually touch the world! And yes, it has already started!

The verse then says that these seven will be glad when they see the plumb line in the hand of Zerubbabel. In this season the Lord is drawing a line in the sand. Unfortunately, it will only be a remnant that responds to this call for holiness. The seven are the seven spirits of God (Isaiah 11:2) that are waiting to be poured out in all their fullness upon the church. They will be glad when the church government, the leaders of the churches, begin preaching repentance which will lead to the mountains becoming plains. They will be glad because the Holy Spirit is longing to see the imperfect done away with so the fullness can come. 1 Corinthians 13 tells us that currently we are living in a time of manifestations of the Spirit. We know in part and prophesy in part and we see manifestations of the Spirit here and there. We get so excited about the manifestations and we are blessed by them but a little dab will not do it anymore. We need the fullness! When righteousness comes we will see the Body operating in the fullness of the Spirit of wisdom and understanding and knowledge and power. The Body will operate like Jesus did and then some. We will finally fulfill our destiny found in Romans 8:29 which tells us that we were predestined to be conformed to the image of Christ. We are supposed to look like Him in every aspect. We are to love perfectly like He loved. We are to have perfect intimacy with the Father like He had (see also John 17:21), perfect compassion, perfect power to witness, heal, and cast out demons, and perfect purity of heart. How can this be? It will not be of us, again it will be by His grace to those who wake up and believe it can happen!

This information and revelation to Zechariah was all well and good, just as it is to us. But if we are hungry, we want to know what Zechariah wanted to know: What do the olive trees represent? How can we get the unceasing flow of oil? Zechariah was so hungry at this point he was probably ready to explode! Finally Zechariah says in verse twelve: "Enough already! You have got to tell me about these two olive trees! I want the ceaseless flow, I beg you, give me the revelation!" In what probably seemed like a cruel joke to Zechariah, the angel remained silent. We must keep asking, seeking, and knocking desperately for God to give us a Word that will bring the flow. The hungry will get the revelation because they persevere in prayer and in hunger. Sure enough, the angel finally answered:

"And he answered me, Do you not know what these are? And I said, No, my lord. Then said he, These are the two sons of oil [Joshua the high priest and Zerubbabel the prince of Judah, the two anointed ones] who stand before the Lord of the whole earth [as His anointed instruments]." (Zechariah 4:13-14)

Wow! What a revelation! If we would walk in these two anointings, we, too, will see a continuous flow of oil. We must walk in the Kingly (Governmental) anointing and the Priestly anointing. We are Kings and Priests. We are a Kingdom of priests. We are a royal priesthood. We come from the line of Jesus who came in the order of Melchizedek who was a King and Priest! These two anointings are two sides of the same coin. We cannot walk in one at the exclusion of the other or we will get only squirts of oil. We must know and understand and walk in these anointings and we will experience the unending flow of oil! So as we understand how to walk as kings and priests, we will see Zechariah's vision fulfilled in our day!

Let's take a closer look at some parts of Zechariah four and then look deeper into what the kingly and priestly entail.

Chapter 2: By My Spirit Says the Lord

On my first ministry trip to Pakistan, the Lord gave me a word as to the key to revival in that nation! I will share that word at the end of this book. After sharing that word with them, revival broke out and it has not ceased!! We saw so many miracles that week. At the last meeting, several words of knowledge were given and then the Lord told me to not pray for them but to have the children come forward and pray for them. He told me that they needed to realize it was not us that healed but the power of the Holy Spirit that was available to all! So for each word of knowledge people responded and came forward for prayer. We taught the children a simple prayer model. We told them to say, "Come Holy Spirit!" Then they were to command the healing by saying, "Be healed in Jesus Name!" Then they were to simply ask the person. "How do you feel?" Every person the children prayed for was healed! 100% healings! The last word of knowledge, though, was much more challenging. The word was heart disease. Two pastors responded to that word of knowledge and came forward for prayer. Because this disease was the most "difficult," the Lord told me to call forth the youngest children to come pray. The Lord wanted to further demonstrate that it is not by might, not by power, but by My Spirit. So, I called the youngest children to come forth. No one came. There was a little two-year-old boy in the front row and so I kept motioning for him to come forward but he would not come up. After a minute or two of coaxing with the boy not responding, I saw out of the corner of my eye a stirring on the other side of the sanctuary. I looked over and saw several mothers bringing up their babies so they could pray for the two men! I realized I had asked for the youngest children to come forth! I have to admit, their faith was greater than mine. So, I told the mothers to position the babies to lay their hands on the two men. One of the babies whose name was Angelica (she is the Pastor's daughter and was being held by the Pastor's wife) reached out her five-month-old hands and placed them directly on one of the Pastors' heart. Other babies laid hands on the other Pastor. Because the babies could not pray, I prayed, "Come Holy Spirit, be healed in Jesus Name!" Then I asked the men how they felt. Both Pastor's came up on the platform. The first Pastor testified he had been in heart pain for several days but as soon as that baby laid hands on him he felt what was like cold rushing water go through his body and he was instantly healed! The other Pastor was also instantly healed. It is not by our might! The presence and power of the Holy Spirit is alive and well and available to all! Baby Angelica as well as her older sisters go around and are still healing the sick! A ceaseless flow of the Spirit of God is available to all!!

So back to our passage so all can experience this flow, these rivers of living water! Let's break down Zechariah 4 section by section to understand the extremely important principles that we must know in order to experience this flow. Let's begin by taking a closer look at v. 6 and v. 10. These verses reveal the importance of the anointing, the oil, the Holy Spirit, and the seven eyes of the Lord.

Verse 6 of Zechariah four is the most famous verse, and one of the most important.

"Then he said to me, This [addition of the bowl to the candlestick, causing it to yield a ceaseless supply of oil from the olive trees] is the word of the Lord to Zerubbabel, saying, Not by might, nor by power, but by My Spirit [of Whom the oil is a symbol], says the Lord of hosts." Zechariah 4:6 AMP

I knew this verse in my head but did not have it in my spirit man until July of 2002. I had been seeking a deeper move of the Lord in my life and I went to a "Word, Spirit, and Power" conference led by Charles Carrin, Jack Taylor, and R.T. Kendall. Being a Baptist and having somewhat of an "attitude" toward charismatics, I was immediately put on the defensive when I realized the church hosting the conference was probably of that persuasion when the worship leader began worship with the words, "Are you ready to receive?" After having a discussion about this with the Lord (instead of worshipping), I finally concluded to Him that I came to give, not receive, because I loved Him and lovers give. I am sure He was impressed with my mega spiritual conclusion, or at least I thought He was until He responded back to my heart, "Thank you that you love Me and that you want to give to Me, but don't you think I love you and that I would like to give to you?" I answered in my heart that I knew He loved me. But I was taken back by Him saying that He might want to give me something. Up to that point my life was all about works, about doing, about serving. But after letting that thought sink in, I finally told Him that I believed He did want to give me something because He loved me. Immediately He answered back to me, "THEN ARE YOU READY TO RECEIVE?!!" I knew then that the Lord was going to move in my life in a new way. To make a long story short, that night the Lord told me that if I walked forward at the end of the service the preacher, Charles Carrin, was going to lay hands on me and that I would fall down on the ground (which I had seen people do at other conferences hosted by charismatics but never seemed to work for me). So I did go down to the altar, he did lay hands on me, I did fall down, and I did not know it then, but I had "received" the baptism of the Holy Spirit. I eventually got up off of the floor, sat down at my seat, and after the conference was completed, I went home. The next Sunday I got up to preach and I preached the same way I always had, I prepared the same way, same delivery style, to the same people. After the message, though, some people came up to me and asked me what had happened to me. I did not realize it until then, but I had preached for the first time under the anointing of power and it was very noticeable to the people as to the difference in my message. I came to understand that it is not by might, not by power, but by the Spirit that we must walk to be effective in ministry. Within weeks I was seeing people healed and delivered instantly at church! Now I have learned to trust the anointing, trust the Holy Spirit, be led of the Spirit, and allow Him the freedom to work through me. I can't earn a powerful message, I can't trust a certain delivery style or preparation method, and I can't count on what worked last week to work this week. I must be led of the Spirit and trust His power in me to take over and as I have learned to do that since that night in June, my ministry has moved from being in the flesh to being in the Spirit. Oh, that it would be a ceaseless flow of the Holy Spirit for all of us rather than a few powerful messages or miracles here and there!

It is by the anointing and only by the anointing that we will get anything done for the Kingdom. If we can only get to the place where we are always trusting the anointing, every minute of every day, we will be led of the anointing, led of the Spirit, and we will see a ceaseless flow of oil. The result? According to Romans 8, the manifestation of the sons of God! Also, what good is a ceaseless flow of the oil of the Spirit if we do not trust the oil or walk in the oil or be led of the oil of the Spirit?

Let's look closer at Romans 8 as it gives us insight as to the importance of a deep move of the Holy Spirit in these last days. Let's look at Romans 8:13-29:
*"For if you live according to [the dictates of] the flesh, you will surely die. But if through **the power of the [Holy] Spirit** you are [habitually] putting to death (making extinct, deadening) the [evil] deeds prompted by the body, you shall [really and genuinely] live forever. For all who are **led by the Spirit of God are sons of God**. For [the Spirit which] you have now received [is] not a spirit of slavery to put you once more in bondage to fear, but you have received the Spirit of adoption [the Spirit producing sonship] in [the bliss of] which we cry, Abba (Father)! Father! **The Spirit Himself [thus] testifies** together with our own spirit, [assuring us] that we are children of God. And if we are [His] children, then we are [His] heirs also: heirs of God and fellow heirs with Christ [**sharing His inheritance with Him**]; only we must **share His suffering if we are to share His glory**. [But what of that?] For I consider that the*

*sufferings of this present time (this present life) are not worth being compared with **the glory that is about to be revealed to us and in us and for us and conferred on us**! For [**even the whole] creation (all nature) waits expectantly and longs earnestly for God's sons to be made known** [waits for the revealing, the disclosing of their sonship]. For the creation (nature) was subjected to frailty (to futility, condemned to frustration), not because of some intentional fault on its part, but by the will of Him Who so subjected it—[yet] with the hope That nature **(creation) itself will be set free from its bondage to decay and corruption** [and gain an entrance] into the glorious freedom of God's children. We know that the whole creation [of irrational creatures] has been **moaning together in the pains of labor until now. And not only the creation, but we ourselves too**, who have and enjoy the **firstfruits of the [Holy] Spirit** [a foretaste of the blissful things to come] groan inwardly as we wait for the redemption of our bodies [from sensuality and the grave, which will reveal] our adoption (our manifestation as God's sons)... So too the **[Holy] Spirit comes to our aid and bears us up in our weakness**; for we do not know what prayer to offer nor how to offer it worthily as we ought, but the **Spirit Himself goes to meet our supplication and pleads in our behalf** with unspeakable yearnings and groanings too deep for utterance... We are assured and know that [God being a partner in their labor] all things work together and are [fitting into a plan] for good to and for those who love God and are called according to [His] design and purpose. For those whom He foreknew [of whom He was aware and loved beforehand], He also **destined from the beginning [foreordaining them] to be molded into the image of His Son** [and share inwardly His likeness], that He might become the firstborn among many brethren."* (Romans 8:13-29 AMP)

It is by His very Holy Spirit that not only will we see a last great outpouring, but it will literally effect all of creation. Can you imagine all the inward groaning that is occurring in people's lives now due to hurt, heartache, financial difficulties, unresolved personal issues, family crises, and on and on? Their groaning goes before the Lord

24/7 and has for thousands of years. We cannot imagine all the hurt but we have the answer! Throw into that equation that the earth itself is groaning, waiting for its redemption, waiting to be restored to the state it had in the Garden. Creation was never intended to bear thorns and thistles and to be dry and parched or be frozen wasteland or flooded or full of hurricanes and tornadoes and earthquakes and tsunamis. The rocks, trees, ground, and oceans are inwardly groaning and crying out for their redemption as well. Everyone and everything is waiting for the flow of the Spirit to begin. If we can just walk in the Spirit, be led of the Spirit, trust the anointing, get out of the flesh, all of mankind will notice as will all of creation! If that is not enough, there are other incredible truths of Scripture in this passage that will come to pass. We will begin to walk in our inheritance! We will begin to share His glory! His glory will not only rise among us, but it will be on us and people will come to its light (see also Isaiah 60:1-3)! Our prayers will be powerful as the Holy Spirit intercedes through us! And what may be the most incredible promise of all, we will finally walk in our destiny! This passage says we were "pre-destinied" to be conformed into the very likeness of Jesus. Do you want the character of Jesus? His love? His power? His oneness with the Father? As we enter into this move of a ceaseless flow of oil that will lead us, we will finally fulfill our destiny to be like Jesus, to literally receive the fullness of God. Verse 1 of Zechariah 4 affirms this as it says that the candlestick is made of gold which represents God's nature. We will come into the very nature of God Himself. 2 Peter 1:4 promises us that we will become partakers of His divine nature. Oh, for the Body of Christ to become spotless, conformed to Christ's image, and walking in the very nature of God Himself! Let it be Lord! May we move in the Spirit and get out of our own strength and power and allow Him to move us into a Body that looks and acts like Him!

Zechariah says that it will not be about our might or power. It will not be about our personalities, programs, our big name conference speakers, or by the works of our hands. It must be about the Anointing, The Holy Spirit is the anointing. He is the Oil. Without the oil, there is no hope for a last days revival, There is no hope for a massive evangelistic harvest. There is no hope for anything. With a little oil, there is a little hope. With a lot of oil, there is a lot of hope. With a ceaseless flow of oil, there is a ceaseless flow of hope! We must see the kingly and priestly open the doors for this flow to be released and then we just trust the anointing and be led of the Spirit!

In verse 10, we find that the "seven eyes" of the Lord will rejoice when the plumb line is in the hand of Zerubbabel. When the government or leadership of the church begins to preach repentance from works of the flesh and begins to preach how to be led of the Spirit, the seven-fold Holy Spirit will rejoice. The Holy Spirit knows that the heights of revival are based on the depths of repentance. There will be no ability to move into the required holiness for this season without God's grace. What are the seven eyes of the Spirit? How do they fit in to the end times revival? Isaiah 11:2 defines the seven-fold Holy Spirit this way: *"And the Spirit of the Lord shall rest upon Him—the Spirit of wisdom and understanding, the Spirit of counsel and might, the Spirit of knowledge and of the reverential and obedient fear of the Lord."* How about a ceaseless flow of wisdom, understanding, counsel, might or power, knowledge, and the fear of the Lord. Are you getting the picture yet of the potential of the last great outpouring that will be unstoppable? We will get to the practical part of what it will take to see this flow happen in the last three chapters of this book, but before we do, we must believe the vision of what it should look like. Only when we see the scope of what the Lord wants to do will we get hungry enough to pay the price to see it happen.

Another passage may be of interest here, Acts 2:17-21. This passage tells us what it will look like when the Holy Spirit is poured out. The first thing that happens is the prophetic. Sons and daughters will prophesy, different age groups will have dreams and visions. God will be no respecter of gender, menservants and maidservants will prophesy. This is important because Revelation 19:10 tells us that the Spirit of Jesus is the Spirit of prophecy. We will know that we are moving in the right direction toward revival and Christlikeness when the prophetic breaks forth in the Body. Then the passage says that signs and wonders will come, then many will be saved. This is the exact picture of Jesus' ministry. He started His ministry by the announcement of the Prophet, John the Baptist, then as He began to preach and teach signs and wonders abounded, then people were saved. We should expect to see this same pattern when the ceaseless flow of oil is poured out on the Body.

There are two major hindrances to walking in the Spirit that I would like to share. In the last days there will be and is already a spirit of anti-Christ that will dominate many sectors of Christianity. This spirit is anti-Christ or anti-anointing. This spirit is against the gifts of the Spirit, is against miracles, signs, and wonders, is against deliverance, and is especially against the gift of tongues. In my early ministry years as a youth pastor and a pastor I faced this demonic force almost daily. I was so hungry for more but those around me walked in this spirit and did everything, including dedicating whole books, to call "the anointing" heresy. Seeking Him will break through the anti-Christ spirit because everyone who seeks, finds, all who knock, the door is open, all who ask, receive.

The second major obstacle is religion. Galatians 4:21-31 tells us that we are led by the Promise, not by our fleshly ideas. The story of Sarah and Hagar illustrate this truth perfectly. God gave Abraham a Promise. When it was slow in manifesting, Abraham and Sarah decided to "help" God in the process and Ishmael was conceived by Sarah's handmaid Hagar. Our efforts in helping God out are all religion. Our ideas as to how to grow our churches or ministries are all religion. God is not looking for us to come up with great ideas, He is not looking for us to run the programs that worked for another church, He is not looking for us to brainstorm, and He is certainly not obligated to bless today what worked yesterday. Those things are all religion. We are to be led of the Spirit daily and even moment by moment! One can grow a church, a ministry, or a business with just a good mind and good administration and leadership. But whatever is birthed by flesh will only yield flesh and will only continue with flesh. That is a major reason cities are not changing while some churches are growing. We must get a Promise from God, then we get a strategy as to how to see the Promise fulfilled, then we walk in the Spirit with patience and obedience until the Promise is manifested! For Abraham it was many years. For us it may be years, months, or days, but we must allow perseverance to do its work. The way to deal with this spirit of religion is to obey verse 30, cast out the bondwoman and her son! The children of Hagar (those who walk in religion) will be more than those who are led of the Spirit and will even persecute those who are led of the Spirit (vv. 27, 29). Even so, we must cast out religion and its effect on future generations. We as a church repented of religion, made a decree to cast out Hagar and her son, and we promptly lost many in our church that were under the control of a spirit of religion. It was hard to see people we loved so much taken out by that spirit. Yet, that was the beginning of great moves of power and revelation by the Holy Spirit as we began the journey of always being led of the Holy Spirit!

Chapter 3: The Power of God's Grace and Favor

Let's move on now to verse 7. It declares that the obstacles we face in possessing this oil will be overcome by God's grace or with shouts of "Grace, grace" to them. We are in a season where we not only need the grace of God, but we need a double portion of it! We need grace, grace! We need grace and peace multiplied to us (1 Peter 1:2, 2 Peter 1:2) We need mega grace (Acts 4:33, great grace). We need to be highly favored or graced (Luke 1:28, Eph. 1:6 accepted or highly favored, *charitow*). In order to see the ceaseless flow of oil, we must understand grace and its power. The late Del Fehsenfeld, founder of Life Action Ministries, defined grace as God giving us the desire and power to do what He would have us to do. That definition changed my life. I realized that if God's grace was at work in me, then even when I did not feel like obeying, He would give me the desire to obey and if I did not have the power to obey, He would give me the power. This is confirmed in Philippians 2:13 that says that it is God who works in us both to will (to desire) and to work (have the strength or power) for His good pleasure. If we could tap into that grace, there is nothing we could not do and no obstacle could stop us! Aren't you glad we have a covenant of grace and a promise that we can go to the throne of grace and get all the grace, help and mercy we need at any time of day or night for any need we have? Let's examine what grace is for, how we get grace, and what hinders grace from being released to us. Without grace, grace, there will be no ceaseless flow of oil. The opposite of grace is works. We have a promise of rest from our works. In other words, we live in the dispensation of grace. We cannot work to earn anything. EVERYTHING in the Kingdom of God is a gift to be received and then released! Freely we receive, then freely we can give. We can do all things through Christ who strengthens us because of His grace. Let' see what God's grace, which was released to us at the cross, has made available to us.

<u>What grace can do for us</u>:

1. Grace releases salvation (Ephesians 2:8-9). What a great truth! To think that we cannot and will not be saved unless the Lord Himself reaches down and gives us the desire to be saved and the power to be saved. To think that there could be cries of grace, grace to lost people and they would come to the Lord in droves! Let us begin shouting grace, grace to the obstacles that keep the unsaved from being born again. Then we will watch the harvest begin to be brought in. This is key for these last days as we should expect an end times harvest according to Jesus. Praise the Lord for this truth! Unfortunately, this is about the only thought most of us have about grace. Grace gives us so great a salvation but that is only the beginning! Let's look at other things grace does for us.

2. Grace gives us the desire and power to do all things in the Christian life (Phil 2:13), and it is available in greater and greater measure (Acts 4:33, James 4:6, 2 Peter 3:18), so nothing is impossible with God!!! Thus, grace one of the main keys and main resources God gives us in the Christian life. Grace also means favor or success. *Declare grace and favor and success DAILY over your life and the life of your family and the lives of those you minister to*!!!!

3. Grace releases miracles (Acts 4:33, 6:8, 14:3). Grace can be ON us! Notice the key to the signs and wonders were men and women of God that were full of grace. Acts 4:33 compliments Zechariah by revealing that the key to the disciples success was

the mega or great grace that was on them. In a time when miracles, signs and wonders are critical to outreach, we must walk as kings and priests and shout grace, grace and watch a ceaseless flow of the miraculous mark our ministries. Also, personally we can shout grace, grace to a situation that needs a miracle!

4. Grace releases abundance (2 Cor. 9:6-8). So many struggle financially when the Bible talks so much about the Lord meeting all of our needs. Grace is the key to abundance. Look at v. 8 in the Amplified translation: *"And God is able to make all grace (every favor and earthly blessing) come to you in abundance, so that you may always and under all circumstances and whatever the need be self-sufficient [possessing enough to require no aid or support and furnished in abundance for every good work and charitable donation]."* According to this passage, we should not only have all of our needs met, but we should have plenty left over to meet the needs of others. Shout grace, grace to your financial situation!

5. Grace releases revival (Ezra 9:7-9 NASB). Do we need a little reviving in this nation? Yes, more than ever. Not only will His grace give revival, but also a peg into the Holy of Holies, a remnant that changes the world, and supernatural revelation. If you desire revival in this hour, begin shouting grace, grace to yourself, your family, your church, your community and your nation!

6. Grace releases wisdom (Ephesians 1:7-8). A whole series of books could be written on the importance of getting and having wisdom. The whole book of Proverbs is dedicated to the pursuit of wisdom. Grace releases wisdom and wisdom releases prosperity in every aspect of life. Wisdom was with God at the beginning and must be with us now. Nothing eternal will happen without wisdom. The Holy Spirit is called the Spirit of

Wisdom and Paul prayed that the Ephesians have a spirit of wisdom and revelation and for the Colossians to have the Spirit of wisdom and understanding. The Body of Christ is in desperate need of wisdom in this hour in the midst of a world that sorely lacks it so call out to the throne of grace for more grace for wisdom.

7. Grace allows us to rule and reign with Christ (Romans 5:17)! We are kings and priests that have been given authority to reign here as Christ's re-presentatives. In order to reign with Him and for him, we daily need His grace. According to this passage, all we need to do is receive that grace!!

8. Grace releases prudence (Ephesians 1:7-8). This is similar to wisdom except prudence is the ability to make the right decisions in life. How many big decisions do we make per day, per week, per month, or per year. Can't we look back at the times when we wished we would have made a different decision? With prudence, we have the practical ability to make the right decisions at the right precise time. Lord, please give us multiplied grace for more prudence!

9. Grace releases redemption (Ephesians 1:7). We have already seen that grace brings salvation, but salvation is just a part of redemption. We were redeemed from every curse through the blood of Jesus. This redemption was made available by the riches of His grace. So when we come under attack from sickness, disease, poverty, sin, or even death, we can shout grace, grace to those things because we have been redeemed from every curse. God's grace truly is amazing! Do not suffer from these curses another minute of your life. The blood covenant of grace eradicated them. Walk in the blessing, not the curse!

10. Grace releases peace and strength and perfection when weak and discouraged (2 Thess. 2:16, 2 Cor. 12:9-10, 4:15-18, Matt.

8:24-26, 1 Peter 5:10, Phil. 1:19, supply: special abundant supply of the HS when I am completely bankrupt of it). One of the greatest weapons the enemy is using in these days is discouragement. When we get discouraged, we lose strength. When we lose strength, we lose joy. When we lose joy, we lose hope. We desperately need grace at this hour to overcome discouragement and weakness. When you are experiencing the spirit of heaviness, begin to praise and call out grace, grace to your circumstances!

11. Grace releases holiness (Titus 2:11-12, Romans 5:17, Psalm 119:32 AMP). This should be life transforming. Realize that you could not save yourself, you needed God's grace for salvation. The same grace that saved you is the grace that teaches you holiness! You can't save yourselves nor can you sanctify yourself. But just as you were saved when you least deserved it, you will be sanctified and made holy by His grace as well. I have personally on numerous occasions not felt like doing what was right, but when tempted I knew I could call upon God's grace and so I did. It was amazing how the grace would flow to me from heaven and I felt immediately the desire and power to obey. For some that are facing major sin issues such as addictions or even worse, understand that when you are weak, He is strong, and that the grace of God is so powerful it can overcome even the deep darkness that will be displayed in the last days according to Isaiah 60:2. Shout grace, grace over your life when you are struggling with sin issues and watch God teach you how to be holy! Watch vile sinners saved and watch believers who are desperately struggling with sin have the grace to overcome when this great grace is released. Even the Psalmist understood that God gives us a willing heart to obey by His grace. How much more so in the covenant of grace! Romans 5:17 reminds us that this abundant grace needs only to be received!

12. Grace releases salvation and boldness to be a witness

(Ephesians 2:8-9, Acts 4:31-33, 15:11). We all know about God's grace for salvation but how often do we shout grace, grace towards lost people? They are not saved by our expert witnessing techniques, they are saved by grace in spite of what we think are expert witnessing techniques! Let God's grace give you boldness and courage and the correct witness for each person and we will see an outbreak of salvations! God's grace through you will do more in a few minutes than hours of witness training can ever do.

13. Grace releases our callings and destinies (Gal. 1:15-16). What are you going to be when you grow up? Some still do not know their destiny and calling after many years of knowing the Lord. You will not find your calling in a spiritual gift inventory, you will find it in the grace of God. Quit searching for a calling, search for Him. Allow His grace to manifest at the right time and reveal to you your destiny. Shout grace, grace to your destiny!

14. Grace grows us up and builds us up in order to receive our inheritance (1 Corinthians 3:10, Acts 20:32, Psalm 119:5-6 AMP)! Paul called himself a master builder. He was able to build up the body so well because it was God's grace that allowed him to do so. We all need to be built up, to grow up. We also hear a lot about receiving our inheritance. We will receive nothing without His grace. Count on the Lord to give you your inheritance and to build you up with shouts of grace, grace to it! In Psalm 119, the psalmist knew he needed something to help him obey. He was under the law and not under grace so he was searching for what we have in our better covenant! As we receive that help, that grace, we will not fail to receive or inherit the promises!!

15. Grace releases us to mend broken relationships, maintain healthy ones, and create networking relationships of favor that we need to fulfill our destiny (Heb. 12:15, Philippians 1:7)! One key to end times victory will be unity in the Body of Christ (see

John 17:21). If the enemy can get us to just avoid our enemies instead of reconciling with them, the world will never be reached. One of the hardest and most humbling things in the Christian walk is to humble oneself and reconcile a relationship. If you do not have the desire or power to do it, shout grace, grace to it and watch the Lord move you with compassion and a deep desire to get it right. Through the years I have stuck my foot in my mouth at best and said and done terrible things to others at worst. To try to bring myself to humbly right those relationships was impossible for me. It was too humiliating and embarrassing. But when I learned about grace and started asking for it to right those relationships, I had the desire and power to confront those people and make right those relationships. I can now honestly say that there is no one in the world that I know of that I am out of relationship with as far as it depends on me. What peace that brings! Your relationships will be powerfully and wonderfully restored as well when grace, grace is poured out on you! You will also find that the grace that mends relationships is also the power that keeps good relations from going sour or bitter. With God's grace, you will find God connecting you with people that create opportunities for favor in fulfilling your ministry and destiny just as God opened the door for Paul to minister to the Philippians through a vision. You will "accidentally" run into someone who holds the key to opening the door you have been praying for to be opened just as David accidentally ran into the Egyptian servant of those who had just burned Ziklag and kidnapped their wives and children (1 Samuel 30:7-20)! You will happen upon someone with the financial means to support your vision. God will strengthen you in the area of love and compassion and that will open doors for miraculous ministry to individuals and groups that otherwise are not seeing breakthrough just as Philip did at Samaria (Acts 8:4-8). You will have a breaker anointing because of the mega grace on you and you will be established with those people in a wonderful new relationship!

16. Grace releases worship and the glory (2 Cor. 4:15, Col. 3:16). Colossians says to sing with thankfulness in our hearts. The word is actually grace in the Greek. It is grace that allows us to sing and praise and worship. Thanksgiving will also release multitudes glorifying the Lord. Worship will be another end times key, so worship with shouts of grace, grace!

17. Grace releases spiritual gifts (Rom. 1:11). This is similar to our callings and destinies. You will not find your spiritual gifts in an inventory, you will find them in the midst of ministry. Opportunities will come your way to minister and when you think you are not gifted to fulfill that ministry, shout grace, grace to it and you will have all the grace, power, and giftedness you need from the Lord to make a miraculous difference. Also we should be aware that Paul was eager to lay hands on the body of Christ to impart spiritual gifts. When was the last time you had an apostolic leader in the body lay hands on you in order to receive grace?

18. Grace gives us favor with God and man (Luke 2:52, Acts 2:47)! Anytime you see the word favor in Scripture, you can interchange it with the word grace. Grace is favor! The Old Testament is full of people that "found favor with God." Whenever they found favor with God, miraculous and awesome blessings came their way. If only we could find favor with God today, we would see the same miraculous and awesome blessings in an even greater measure. Guess what, you have found favor with God!!! Ephesians 1:6 tells us that we have not only found favor with God through Jesus, but we are highly favored. To be *"accepted"* in the beloved is the same word used of Mary, *charitow*, which means highly favored. We are as highly favored as Mary, the mother of Jesus, was! With shouts of grace, grace, expect to be highly favored at home, at work, in your ministry, in your finances, in your health, in every area of your life. No obstacle can stand before you, they will all fall and become a plain because of God's grace, grace and favor, favor

on your life!! Psalm 5:12 says that favor surrounds us as a shield! Grace protects us from the attacks of the enemy and turns every attack into God's favor!!! Psalm 41:11 says, *"By this I know that You favor and delight in me, because my enemy does not triumph over me."* If we can catch hold of this revelation of grace and favor, our world will be totally and completely turned upside down and right side up! You will see yourself for who you really are, one who is always led in triumph by His grace and one who is more than a conqueror at all times because of His favor. You will always win because He won at the cross! The game was finished and victory and grace were released! Now we just walk in it as we receive grace on a moment by moment basis! If that is not enough, we even grow in grace and go from grace to grace and have grace multiplied to us! The closer we draw to Jesus, the more grace is given! Wow! What a covenant! To Jesus be all the glory, to the praise of His glorious grace!!

19. After going through the shaking and receiving the Kingdom that cannot be shaken, grace then allows us to serve Him and walk with Him acceptably (Heb. 12:27-28). Grace is the good news, the shaking is the bad news! In the end, allow the Lord to shake you to your core so anything that is not of the Kingdom of God is shaken out and there is nothing left but grace! All that you have trusted in, your works, talents, ideas, programs, worldly wisdom, personality, and etc., will be shaken out and you will realize that you cannot put any trust in them lest you have reason to boast. There is one thing to boast in, that is Jesus Christ and Him crucified, dead, and resurrected, lavishing His grace upon us! Then, with all of the old covenant of works gone, with all worldliness gone, we can receive a Kingdom that cannot be shaken because we shout grace, grace and serve Him with powerful effectiveness and also please Him by walking acceptably.

20. Grace overcomes obstacles (Zechariah 4:7). Whenever we have

an issue that comes up that often seems insurmountable (like a mountain in the way, we just need to shout, "Grace, grace" to it and it will fall!

Ways to get grace:

1. Receive it (John 1:16-17, Romans 5:17)! Grace is undeserved, it is a gift, it is to be accepted and received. Of His fullness we have all received, grace upon grace upon grace upon grace! Never ending! Unceasing flow of it! Oftentimes grace comes out of the blue when you least expect it. Your whole attitude changes and the atmosphere changes around you because the Lord pours out some grace upon you. What a God we have that takes care of us like He does. His eyes are always on us. Just as Jesus was full of grace and truth, that is our inheritance as well. Just receive a truckload of grace right now from your loving heavenly Father!

2. Ask for it (Heb. 4:16, 2 Pet. 1:2, Psalm 119:58, also, every letter of Paul begins and ends with a prayer for grace). We are told in Hebrews that we can ask for grace any time of day. This is crucial because we need grace at all times of the day! Scripture describes the throne of Jesus as the throne of grace. Do you think He has enough grace to go around? He has so much grace He died to give it away! When we struggle grace is just a heavenly 911 away!

3. Put a demand on the covenant (John 1:17). We know that we are no longer under the covenant of the Law, we are under a better covenant of grace. When a covenant agreement is made, there are promises to fulfill on both sides. Under the New Covenant of grace we are to give our hearts and lives to Jesus and live for Him by faith. In return, God grants us grace and

mercy to forgive our sins and have peace with God. He even gives us grace to fulfill our end of the agreement, grace to live for Him. On top of that, He gives us everything we need for life and godliness. If that is the agreement, then we should expect God to fulfill His end of the bargain and He should expect us to fulfill ours. If we are walking with Him and we come across a need that He has promised to meet, we can place a legal demand on the blood that sealed the covenant. For example, if I am struggling with a specific sin, I can put a demand on the covenant and call for grace to overcome that sin. God has obligated Himself by covenant to oblige us and give us the grace to overcome any and every sin issue. He will not do it grudgingly, He sent His only Son to shed His blood and die for us in order to get that grace to us! Why would He not release it to us? Later in the chapter will be some grace blockers that can stop the flow of grace to us, but if we are walking with Him, we can put a demand on the covenant and call for grace. We are not under the Law where we have to earn His help. We are under grace where it is given freely. So pray something like this: "Lord, I put a demand on the covenant and request grace for my need (be specific with your need). Thank you that You promised it to me and I receive it right now because You are not a god that would lie. I stand in covenant with You and I access the grace that Jesus died to give me! Thank You, in Jesus Name!"

4. Receive it or access it by faith (Rom. 5:1-2, Titus 2:11-12, Eph. 2:8, John 1:16). We have access to this amazing grace by faith. Like all parts of the Christian life, faith can activate God's plan and in this case, faith can activate God's grace in any and every situation. Believe that God will release grace to you at the moment you need it and you will often times experience that grace immediately! Sometimes He gives us direction as to how to access that grace. Faith without works is dead, so if You receive it by faith and He tells You what to do next, do it! If the Body of Christ got hold of this fact and began to believe God

gives grace, grace through our faith, we would see a ceaseless flow of oil multiply around the world. How do we get the ceaseless flow? By faith! When you boil it down, the ceaseless flow of oil is the ceaseless flow of His grace!

5. Confess it as yours (Romans 10:9-10, Psalm 2:7). We can declare God's decrees. If He has promised us something that means He has decreed it and that decree cannot be broken and it must come to pass. We must loose what He has already loosed in Heaven (Matthew 16:19, 18:18-20). His decrees are written down in Scripture and we need to declare His decrees or loose His promises over ourselves, our families, our churches, our communities and our situations. Declare and decree favor over yourself and your family daily! If God has promised us grace upon grace and favor upon favor, declare His decree! Do not let your children go off to school without declaring God's promised grace and favor over them. Do not let your husband or wife go one day without loosing His mega favor over him or her. Confess you are full of grace (John 1:14), you have great (mega) grace (Acts 4:33), receive abundance of grace (Rom. 5:17), confess more and more grace (2 Cor. 4:15 Message), exceeding grace of God in you (2 Cor. 9:14), the riches of his grace (Eph. 1:7), the exceeding riches of his grace (Eph. 2:7), the grace of our Lord was exceeding abundant (1 Tim. 1:14), more grace (James 4:6), all grace (1 Peter 5:10), true grace of God (1 Peter 5:12), grace and peace be multiplied unto you (2 Peter 1:2), grow in grace (2 Peter 3:18), the grace of God upon you (Luke 2:40), grace upon grace (John 1:16), immeasurable (limitless, surpassing) riches of His free grace, His unmerited favor (Eph. 2:7)!!!!!!!!!!

6. Know Him (2 Peter 1:2-3)! Grace and peace will be multiplied to us through the knowledge of Him. That would be reason enough to get to know Him better each and every day. Of course, we get to know him more because we love Him, but there are great rewards for seeking Him and becoming intimate

with Him. This passage is interesting in that it says we receive grace and peace just like we receive his divine power and everything we need for life and godliness through the knowledge of Him. Can we love Him so much and desire Him so much that He just begins to overflow oil and peace and grace and anointing in return upon the ones He loves? Yes, and in greater measures than we can ask for or imagine, so let's get back to our first focus in life: loving Jesus with all of our heart, soul, mind and strength!

7. Be humble (James 4:6). It is humbling when we recognize that without Him we can do nothing. With Him, nothing is impossible. Why? Because when we humble ourselves and admit our weakness, His grace takes over. When I am weak and humble, He is strong. It is not us, but the grace of God in us that labors. As soon as we begin to think it is us, the Lord will pull back His grace and we will find out real quick what He can do through grace compared to what we can do in the flesh. Sometimes, the Lord will even orchestrate or allow some embarrassing moments to humble us because He knows we are in need of grace. So in our humility, He has a vessel that He can pour His grace into.

8. Walk uprightly (Psalm 84:11). No good thing does He withhold for them that walk uprightly. What is the first thing on the list of good things He gives? His grace! Grace even comes before His glory. As we walk uprightly, we will go from grace to a greater level of grace. How do we walk uprightly? With his grace! He will give us the desire and power to walk uprightly. With every breakthrough we have over sin, He pours out more grace for the next breakthrough.

9. Overcome testing faithfully (1 Peter 2:19-21. Just as Joseph had to endure many years of testing, trials, and tribulations before he was promoted to his place of favor, we, too, will be tested. Count it all joy when those trials come your way because they

are the precursors to favor! Be faithful and obedient through every trial just as Jesus was and the favor of God will manifest in you in powerful ways!

10. Be in submission to all authorities (1 Peter 5:5). This passage is in the same context of humbling ourselves. It is very humbling to submit to anyone but it is God's way. All we have to do is drive down the road and watch how many Christians drive the speed limit and we will find out how much we care about obeying authorities. Or we can go to the parking lots of churches and listen to church members talk ill of their pastors and realize why there is so little grace in the church today. Pastors talk about other pastors all the time they preach "touch not God's anointed." Wives run the household as do many children. Students run the classrooms. God's grace is nowhere to be found until we submit outwardly and inwardly to ALL authorities. A church that is in order, that has a group of people that loves and respects their leadership will be the church that God's hand of grace is on. Submit, serve, build up one another, obey, and watch a grace revival begin to break out!

11. Be encouraged by others (Eph. 4:29). Has anyone ever come up to you out of the blue to pay you a true, heartfelt compliment? Did it change your whole attitude? Of course it did because Paul tells us that encouraging one another actually releases God's grace to the hearer! What an incredible truth! Have you ever had anyone come up to you and fish for compliments? Why do people do that? It is because they are not getting enough encouragement and therefore their grace tank is low or on empty. Somehow we all instinctively know that we need compliments that release grace in order to survive. We must encourage each other more so more grace will abound! Oh to see a church that is positive and encouraging rather than murmuring and complaining! If you see someone struggling in any way, discouraged, lost, financially struggling, or whatever, go to them with an encouraging word and watch God's grace

almost immediately begin to change their perspective and situation. What a resource we have in encouragement. What would happen if families and churches went one whole day doing nothing but being positive and encouraging? Again, a ceaseless flow of oil would begin to be poured out! Grace, grace would be there and obstacles would begin tumbling and even crashing. Be an encourager and release one of the Lord's greatest gifts, His grace, upon the hearer!

12. Impartation (Romans 1:11). Paul longed to go to Rome to lay hands on the body and impart supernatural (pneumatikos) spiritual gifts (charisma) or grace to establish them. In other words, he did not want the Romans to be up and down, wishy washy, roller coaster Christians not established in their callings and destiny. He wanted them established, firm, strong, rock solid. Grace will do that. Leaders, are you laying hands on the saints so they are flooded with grace?

13. Listen to testimonies and stir up grace through remembrance (2 Timothy 1:5-7). Do we want to stir up the grace of God, do we want it to flow, than remember how we got it in the first place. Tell about the incredible times that God in His grace reached out to us when we least deserved it. Tell others about Him and his magnificent grace. You will begin to sense a new strength, His grace will begin to fall on you afresh and anew. It is amazing how testimonies of God's goodness seemingly open the floodgates of God's presence and power. One of the biggest grace givers in my life comes through the reading of biographies of great fathers of the faith. This changed my ministry. I also began reading the book of Acts over and over and books about the revivals throughout history. Such a hunger began to overwhelm me and drive my life. Grace was released from heaven to me as my remembrance was stirred by what God did in the past. I would literally feel like more than a conqueror after reading those books. Do you want to change your circumstances, change the atmosphere of a church

service, change your perspective? Then begin sharing amongst yourselves how God has moved in the past. Then just let the grace of God well up in you and around you. Faith and grace will be poured out and the spiritual atmosphere will change! You will then receive grace, grace to see revival happen today!

14. Ask for, receive and walk in wisdom (Proverbs 3:4, 8:35, James 1:5). King Solomon tells us that in finding wisdom we find favor. We will receive not just favor but also abundant life, prosperity, etc.

15. Do good unto others, especially those who are hurting and oppressed. You will receive favor as your reward! See Proverbs 11:24, Isaiah 1:17-19. There are not many things in life that turn God's head toward us than when we walk with His heart of love toward the poor and oppressed. When you minister love to people, God will bless you with His favor.

16. Be diligent. Ezra 5:8 (AMP), Proverbs 22:9. It seems that the one at work that always receives the promotions and the favor are those that are most diligent. They are there to make the boss or company look good. God works in the same manner. Those who are diligent in seeking Him, serving him, and honoring Him receive the promotion and reward of the Lord.

17. Honor and do good to others. Proverbs 12:2 (NASB). Evil people may advance, but not with favor. Those who seek the good of others have the favor or hand of God on them at all times! Love never fails!

18. Sin (Romans 5:20, 6:1-2). Wow. If this isn't one of the most incredible statements in all of Scripture. When we sin, we can humbly confess our sin and God's grace is loosed. Some of the most incredible outpourings of God's grace in my life have come after I have sinned. It is no wonder that Paul had to add a

warning not to sin so that grace would abound. It is almost as if God so desires us to have grace, to have His desire and power, to have His anointing and favor, to have his ceaseless flow of oil, that we cannot hardly miss it. We should be able to stumble upon it if nothing else. So why are we not experiencing the grace that removes every obstacle in our life?

Grace blockers:

1. Pride (James 4:6-7). God opposes or "stiff arms" the proud. He stands in our way. That is the exact opposite of grace, God coming to our rescue. Verse 7 shows us the key to all humility, submitting ourselves or surrendering ourselves totally and completely to the lord. We do this by confessing all of our sins, by bringing them to the surface so they do not become a stumbling block at the least nor a stronghold at the worst. We then need to repent or change our mind about how we believe about that area of our life. It must come under the authority of God's word. We do not need to ask forgiveness as forgiveness of all sin was given at the cross and appropriated at salvation, but we do need to surrender that area to the Lord and begin to receive grace to change it. We need to get alone with the Lord and allow Him and lay everything out before him and then receive the grace and righteousness of God and stand there. We do not want to focus on being sin conscious, we want to focus on the righteousness and grace available to us through the blood of Jesus. Also, it seems to me that in my life the issue of pride often boiled down to I either had to be right or I had to be better. It didn't matter if I was arguing with a child or competing against a child, I still had to be right or be better. It even overflowed into ministry, I had to be seen as right or as better. The root of all that for me was insecurity. I felt better about myself when right and when seen as better, even if only in my eyes. It will not be until it does not matter what we look like to others, only what we look like to God, that humility takes over and grace abounds. We are not competing with one

another nor are churches competing with one another. I remember going to a church growth luncheon and the consultant asked who our competition was. I started thinking that our biggest competition was the lake that most of our community lived on, as many spent their time skiing, fishing, jet skiing, or swimming. But the consultant was not looking for that type of an answer, he was wondering what other churches were in our area. To him, they were the competition! Let's stop competing to have the best programs, the fanciest buildings, the biggest name speakers, and let's start working together as believers and churches to grow the Kingdom! Who cares who preaches the best and who has the biggest church. It is all done by His grace anyways so we have no reason to boast or act as if we did something. What matters is God's Kingdom, His Manifest Presence, and how much we love Him and love those around us. Our job, then, is to ask God to make us humble and then walk humbly before our God. Only then will that obstacle to grace fall and revival will be right behind.

2. Bitterness rather than forgiveness (Heb. 12:14-16). This is another huge obstacle. A turning point in my life came when I told the secretary to hold my calls and to not let anyone come into my office and I closed the door, got on my face and cried out to the Lord. I was frustrated in the ministry, mostly ineffective, I didn't like my job, and I knew that I was not living out the book of Acts in my ministry. So, on my face before Him, I told Him to either kill me or fill me. The first thing the Lord told me was that I needed to make a phone call and make a relationship right. I did not want to (pride of course), but when I did, it felt like the weight of the world lifted off me. That was until the Lord reminded me of another wrong relationship, then another, then another. Nine months later I finally righted my last wrong relationship. Then God's grace began filling me like I had never experienced before. That was nine of the hardest months of my life, certainly the most humbling, but with bitterness and unforgiveness gone, I was literally a new man

and a new minister. This passage also says that bitterness is one reason immorality abounds in the Kingdom of God. How that works I do not know but that is what the passage says and it is true. How many believers and even leaders have fallen. Could it be because of bitterness in their heart? It very well could. Let us get our relationships right and stem the tide of immorality. It also says that bitterness is easily transferable, defiling others. Bitterness swipes a wide path in the body of Christ, keeping people away from true Biblical unity and definitely away from an outpouring of grace. Leave your gift at the altar now and go make every single relationship right!! I did!! Expect a ceaseless flow of oil and grace with bitterness out of your heart.

3. Not pastoring or covering or looking out for one another (Heb. 12:15). The word diligently in his passage is the Greek work *episkipeo* where we get our work Episcopal or overseer. If we are not diligent, if we are not looking after one another, covering one another, there is great danger of bitterness and strife manifesting. It is amazing how a mediator or mature leader can stop a fight by just giving perspective, knowing that there are three sides to every story - his side, her side, and what really happened. Let's not fail the grace of God, let's allow peacemakers and overseers in our midst, calling upon them before strife breaks out.

4. Nullifying or falling from grace through self-effort. We are either walking by grace or by works, there are no other options (Gal. 2:21, 5:4). The book of Galatians gives a very important truth for today. We must get out of religion and works (Hagar) and be totally led of the Spirit (Sarah). As soon as we get into works, we get out of the realm of grace. If we were saved by grace we must live by grace. We did not earn our salvation nor can we earn His favor, anointings, success, holiness, prosperity, or anything. When we are led of the Spirit we will be absolutely full of grace. We must stop trusting in programs, the way we used to do it, in denominational mandates, in trying what

worked for the successful "wonderchurch" that I just read about, and etc. Just because something worked yesterday or for someone else does not mean that is what the Lord wants for us at this time. I often quote Rick Warren when he said, "If the horse is dead, dismount!" Let us keep in touch with and move by the Holy Spirit, not by programs or even by what worked yesterday or for someone else's church or life. When we trust those things to work, we are no longer trusting the Holy Spirit's fresh manna and direction for today. When we seek to hear from the Lord and then wait until we hear His voice, then we can act upon His Word knowing that no word of God is without power, and His grace will abound, and obedience will result in great blessing.

5. Receive His grace in vain (2 Cor. 6:1-4). Sometimes God gives us the grace we need and then we do not use it. That is receiving His grace in vain. This passage deals with the "acceptable" time of the Lord. The word acceptable is from the root word to receive. We are living in a time of receiving! Let's not stop the flow of grace by receiving in vain. Also, sometimes we experience God's grace and become a stumbling block or offense to others, being a bad witness. We know that His gifts (grace in the Greek) and callings are irrevocable, but wouldn't you sometimes like to personally revoke the anointings of those who use the grace of God for selfish gain and that bring the Kingdom of God into disrepute due to their actions? We are in a time of God releasing His grace and glory in our midst so the level of holiness and accountability must be high, just as in the days of Achan or Ananias and Sapphira. Let's not treat God's incredible grace with vanity or contempt or take it for granted. It is precious and we must treat it so, revering the One who has poured it out on us.

6. Speaking discouraging words instead of encouraging words (Eph. 4:29). It goes to reason that if encouraging words give grace to the hearer, the opposite must be true. If we speak

negatively toward one another, it is a grace sapper. Not too
many things in life can sap the grace out of us faster than
people putting us down. When treated wrongly, not only can
grace be sapped, but it is a slippery slope to bitterness which
further removes the grace from our lives. We must quit
murmuring and complaining about one another to one another.
Let's quit defiling one another and begin giving grace through
positive words of encouragement. Think about it. If you truly
love someone (and we are to love even our enemies), would we
cut them down which may lead to favor being lifted off of their
life? We should desire all to walk in God's grace and favor,
because what happens to them affects us. For they are a part of
our Body if they are saved. If they are not saved, we could
possibly be destroying the very grace they need for salvation.

7. Not loving your enemies (Luke 6:27-36). Jesus asks us what
credit (Greek word for credit is the word for grace) do we get
from loving those who love us. When we love those who are
unlovely, the implication is that grace and favor will be ours. For
anyone who has lived a lifestyle of ministering to the poor or
needy or oppressed, doesn't it seem like they have so much
grace and favor upon their life? Mother Theresa is the prime
example but all around the world this is true. This could be
called one of the great secrets to God's grace and favor because
it is, unfortunately, so rare. Let us reach out to the least of
these with His love and watch God's grace come on us like a
flood.

8. Unbelief. Faith gives us access into this grace (Romans 5:1-2).
One of the biggest attacks of the enemy is to try to get us to
belief that God's grace and favor is not for us or that we have
done something that will cause His favor to be taken away from
us. The only thing that truly pulls the plug on an outpouring of
grace is to not believe it is always available to us. Even if we get
prideful or fall into works, simple repentance and going back to
the throne of grace gets it flowing again. His throne is *made* of

grace! We do not have to fast and pray and read 5.2 chapters of the Bible to earn back favor. It is a gift! Let us go boldly, with faith, to the throne of grace and obtain grace anytime we need it!! Believe and confess that you are highly favored and God's abundant grace is yours.

Although these lists are not exhaustive, just thinking and reading about how great God's grace is should get His grace flowing in our lives! Let's tap into one of the greatest resources we have, sealed by Jesus' blood, His grace! As a matter of fact, let's ask for a ceaseless flow of it!! Shout loudly grace, grace to EVERY obstacle in your life right now! When Joshua and Israel shouted loudly at the obstacle of the great wall around Jericho, it immediately fell. We must do the same with the wonderful gift of grace. Having no grace is like trying to remove a mountain (obstacle) with a spoon. Having grace is like being given a giant bulldozer to tear down the mountain. Having grace, grace, is like being given dynamite that demolishes the mountain or obstacle miraculously in seconds! Imagine that kind of power applied to the obstacles in your life! That double portion of grace is available for these last days. The double portion is absolutely necessary. The things in our lives that need to change will take a double dose of grace. The supernatural power we need to save the lost and transform whole cities will take mega grace as well. Praise God that He is faithful and the supply of grace will be endless to those who are dependent upon it!

Chapter 4: Understanding the Priestly (The Outer Court)

During one of our trips to Pakistan, the weirdest things happened to me. We were done with all the meetings and it had been an amazing week. Thousands had been saved and healed! But as I relaxed on my bed before I began packing to leave, I felt that the Lord was telling me that the main reason I was there that week had not even happened yet. I immediately sent a message to my wife Lisa asking her to get the intercessors praying because the Lord was about to do something and I was clueless as to what it was, especially since there were no more meetings. About thirty minutes after I sent the message, I was still sitting on the bed. Then, out of the blue, something grabbed my right ear and began yanking it! There was no one in the room but me! I could only conclude it was an angel but the angel would not let go (I told you it was weird!). After what seemed like forever but was probably just a minute or two, the angel let go of my ear. I was a little freaked out but immediately began asking the Lord what that was all about! I shared with the team what happened and then the Lord told us that the priests had to be anointed with blood and oil on their right ear, their right thumb, and their right big toe. He then said something that changed everything for us. He said that kings would command this next move of God but priests would carry it! Then He told us we needed to start ordaining priests to carry this end times move! Then the Lord told us to begin right then so I began ordaining the team as priests by anointing their ear, their thumb, and their toe. It was a life changing experience for all of us. Then back at home, we began to ordain our ministry family and others into the priestly calling.

Hopefully your hunger is now like Zechariah's when the angel asked him a few times if he wanted to understand what the key was to the ceaseless flow of oil. We have seen that there is a ceaseless flow of oil that is available in these last days. We have seen that it is a flow of the Spirit and it is a flow of grace. This flow can touch every area of our lives and ministries. The olive trees never quit flowing through the tubes to the candlestick. These trees represented the kingly and the priestly. Of course Jesus was the perfect representation of a King and a Priest, He was even of the order of Melchizadek, who was also a king and a priest. We are called to be a holy nation, a royal priesthood, fulfilling these roles in our day. In order to do this, we need to better understand how to be a king and how to be a priest. Hopefully these next two chapters will aid you in that call and will be absolutely life changing for you as you begin to grow in these two areas which will allow you to begin soaring from glory to glory, faith to faith, and grace to grace. Most of all it will prime the pump for the ceaseless flow of His Manifest Presence in your life!

The passage in the Amplified reads that the two sons of oil are Joshua the High Priest and Zerubbabel the Governor. That is our clue that these two olive trees hold the key to the ceaseless flow. We therefore must look at these two anointings much more in depth. These next two chapters will lay the foundation for understanding the priestly and the kingly. As we begin to walk in both, the oil will begin to flow. Let's begin, as the passage does, with the priestly. If we are all priests, we must know what the role of the priest was and the practical applications of that role for today. Obviously we live in a dispensation of grace and we do not have to go to a priest, we are priests. Jesus was not only a priest He was the High Priest. We are to be conformed to His image so we are to be as the high priest as well, fulfilling the pattern of his ministry. It was the job of the High Priest to minister in the tabernacle. He went through the stations or furnishings of the tabernacle and once a year he entered into the very Holy of Holies. Acts 15:16 tells us that there is coming a day when the tabernacle of David will be rebuilt. It will not need to be rebuilt physically, but it must be rebuilt in us. We are the temple of God, we are His tabernacle or dwelling place. We must have as our goal entering onto the Holy of Holies.

"Therefore, brethren, since we have confidence to enter the holy place by the blood of Jesus, by a new and living way which He inaugurated for us through the veil, that is, His flesh, and since we have a great priest over the house of God, let us draw near with a sincere heart in full assurance of faith, having our hearts sprinkled clean from an evil conscience and our bodies washed with pure water." (Hebrews 10:19-22 NASB)

Since it was the highest privilege of the high priest to enter into the Holy of Holies once a year, it should be our highest privilege to enter into the Holy of Holies not just once a year, but permanently. Jesus' death on the cross resulted in the veil being rent in two giving us 100% access to the Most Holy Place. It was not only a privilege, it was a journey through the tabernacle that had to be walked with incredible reverence and fear of the Lord. It was only on the Day of Atonement, the high holy day, that the priest made the incredible walk into the place of God's dwelling. It was only entered into by the blood that was shed for that occasion. What a glorious truth that the blood has now been shed once and for all so we can have permanent access to Him and His covenant promises. It was at the Ark of the Covenant that the blood was applied to secure the covenant promise of forgiveness to the Israelites. Now all the covenant promises are available, all yes and amen through the blood of Christ. Let's take a look at the journey the high priest made on that day, and as we go, we will apply it to the daily and lifelong journey we make into a covenant relationship with the Father.

There was only one way in to the tabernacle, one door. We, too, can only enter the tabernacle through the Door, Jesus. We must be born again if we are to ever be in relationship with Him. There is no side door, there is no special works one must do, no hoops to jump through, only a decision of the will by grace through faith that allows us through that door. That door is available to all, God is no respecter of persons. Once we have made that decision, we enter into a new Kingdom, a Kingdom of Light, of Power, of Glory, and of His Presence. Unfortunately, when we enter, we enter as new born babies in Christ and we stand in need of maturity. The rest of the tabernacle and its furniture represent the journey all believers must take to grow up into the fullness of Christ. Too many believers come into a saving relationship with Jesus and think that is all there is to the Christian life, and need only to hold on tight to Him until heaven calls. If that is our mindset, we will miss out on all the promises of the Kingdom of heaven on earth. I cannot wait for heaven, the glory will be incredible. But the glory of heaven is also wanting to come to earth so we can experience some of it now. That is why Jesus commanded us to pray that His Kingdom come on earth just as it is in heaven. Why have we settled for anything less? Since we have settled or become comfortable at salvation or at some other point along the journey, the church has fallen asleep and has not experienced the ceaseless flow. Remember in the beginning of chapter four the angel had to awaken Zechariah. We, too, must wake up to the "more" of Christianity. We can no longer afford to put God in a box or draw a line as to how far we will go spiritually.

Before we go into the pattern, we must know that the journey consists of three stages. In the tabernacle and Temple they were called courts, the outer court, inner court, and the Holy of Holies. This triad is symbolized often is Scripture in various ways. These three "stages" of Christian growth are also described as "30-fold, 60-fold, and 100-fold," it is also seen as "good, acceptable, and perfect," "the Way, the Truth, the Life," "children, young men, fathers," "faith, hope, love," "Egypt, the wilderness, the Promised Land," "cleansed, pruned, abiding," "Passover, Pentecost, Tabernacles," "baptism of water, baptism of the Holy Spirit, baptism of fire," and others. This three-fold distinction tells us that we must continue moving forward. This is important because the outer court was uncovered, subject to the weather and day and night. I call that "rollercoaster" Christianity, always up and down and inconsistent depending on the "weather" or circumstances. The inner court, however, was covered and lit by candlelight. That represents a greater level of protection, growth, power and revelation from the Lord. The Holy of Holies was covered as well but was not lit by any light known to man, Scripture says it is lit by the glory of the Lord! This shows us a snapshot of the journey moving from spiritual infancy and childhood to spiritual maturity and glory!

As soon as one enters through the door of salvation, one moved into the outer court. There is a very important lesson to be learned there that will be indispensable for the rest of the journey. The principle is found in Psalm 100. How do we enter through that door into the outer court? We enter His gates with thanksgiving and His courts with praise. This is true whatever court we enter whether it be outer court, inner court, or Holy of Holies. It is interesting that there seems to be a rebirth in the Kingdom of praise and worship. I believe this is very important because there will be no transitioning between courts without it. Frustration, discouragement, and depression lead to a lack of praise, a lack of faith, and therefore a lack of growth. The Israelites did not enter in due to their unbelief. Our belief that there is more makes us desire to begin the process with praise, walk through the process with praise and end the stage with praise.

The first piece of furniture that the priest encountered when entering the tabernacle was the altar of sacrifice. This was where the sacrifices were brought to the priest for various reasons of consecration and/or forgiveness. The animals took the place of the one offering the sacrifice. We know that Jesus is our blood sacrifice so we no longer have to bring animals on our behalf, He died on our behalf. Praise God for that kind of love and sacrifice on our behalf. We are told in Romans 12:1 that we are to be living sacrifices, therefore we are to die to self, crucify the flesh, and be willing to surrender all for Him as He surrendered all for us. We do not die literally, we die spiritually to self. This is the act of surrender. It is often a very painful process of dying to self but without this surrender, there will never be any true, consistent growth spiritually. One reason the Lord seems to be moving on behalf of His people in this season is because there seems to be a resurgence of hunger and thirst for Him. Passions are being ignited for deeper intimacy and growth. Believers know there is more and they are getting violent to take it by force. In order for this hunger to be satisfied, however, we must understand that it is not satisfied or filled until one is emptied. Surrender means we lay down all that is not like Jesus. It is a decision of the will. True surrender says, "Lord, I give You permission to do in me and to me all that it takes to conform me to Christ's image."

When I talk to believers who are stagnating, the first thing I usually ask them is about surrender. That is almost always the problem. Understanding the tabernacle pattern of growth and maturity helps us to better "diagnose" spiritual sickness. If a person is suffering from rollercoaster Christianity it is usually because there are areas of their life that they will not surrender, that they will not crucify. The Bible does not say to try, it says to die. We must die to flesh and to the principles of the world. For example, if one desires to see true Biblical financial blessing, one cannot be greedy or lack generosity. Those things must be surrendered and crucified, placed on the altar, put at the foot of the cross. Only then can those ungodly characteristics be replaced with a heart of a giver which is the key to Biblical financial blessing. Another example is that one may desire to walk in powerful ministry but does not want to deal with an unloving personality. That ministry will fall apart quickly. These are obvious examples but each of us must say as Paul said, that he was crucified with Christ and he no longer lived, but the life he lived he lived through Christ. Christ will not manifest through us if we choose to stay in the flesh. My life changed with a simple prayer. I told the Lord that I was not even exactly sure what surrender fully meant but that I wanted to surrender all to Him. Shortly after that prayer God began to move on my life to begin to conform me into Christ's image. If the Lord had moved upon me before I prayed that prayer and made that commitment to Him, I would have given up when the fire began to cleanse me. The heights of revival are dependent upon the depths of repentance, but the depths of repentance are dependent upon the heights of surrender. How far will we go? Will we forsake all? The act of surrender may be a simple prayer, but it will have life changing effects. If not surrendered, we will never endure the cleansing that is coming at the next piece of furniture, the bronze laver.

True surrender puts us on the altar as a living sacrifice. True surrender says I will put off the old me and put on the new Him. True surrender says though He slay me, I will trust Him. True surrender is actually total submission to the Lordship or rulership of Christ in your life. A Christian is part of the Kingdom of God and therefore submits to the King of that Kingdom. The believer submits to the King's domain or the King-dom. Lack of true surrender or submission is why 90% of believers are still in the outer court, content with hanging on until Jesus comes. Lack of true surrender is why we hear Christians excusing their sinfulness by saying, "That is just the way I am." Are you willing to allow the Lord to kill you in order to fill you? Are you willing to let your dream die so God can give you His dream for you? Are you tired of little to no fruit that remains? Are you tired of your sin habits? Are you tired of impotent Christianity? The path to true Holy of Holies effectiveness must go through the cross, death to self. Ask the Lord for Him to show you any area of your life that is unsurrendered, that you will not allow Him to touch. Trust me, if it is not surrendered now, it will be exposed later. You are only as strong as your weakest link, surrender your strengths and your weaknesses. That area of surrender may be all that is keeping you from moving from unfruitfulness to bearing much fruit to Your Father's glory.

That simple act of surrender will have lifelong results. You will be giving permission to the Holy Spirit to reveal to you at any time and in any way the obstacles that fleshliness, worldliness, wrong mindsets, or even demonic strongholds are in your life. That one prayer of surrender moved me past the altar of surrender to the Bronze Laver. It was there that the results of my act of surrender began to manifest. Not too long after I had surrendered to the Lord with that simple prayer the Lord began to move upon me with a holy restlessness. The only way to describe it would to be that I became dissatisfied with everything about my life. I disliked ministry, I felt like a failure, I struggled in my marriage, the Bible became boring, my spiritual disciplines became burdensome, I wanted to change churches, I struggled raising my children right, financially I was miserable and discontent, and my face and actions and attitude showed it! I became a complainer and a murmurer, I blamed all those around me for my failures, I talked about or gossiped about everyone from my friends to my Pastor, and I was frustrated with God for putting me in the situations I was in. How is that for the blessing of surrender! I remember things coming to a head one night in an argument with my wife when I got so mad I took the cup full of soda I was drinking and chucked it through the kitchen. It hit the shade covering the window and the drink flew all over it, leaving stains on it for a few years. Then I walked out of the house down our long driveway into the night. I realized I was becoming miserable. The Christian life, I reasoned, was not supposed to be like what I was experiencing. Something had to give. Because I had surrendered, I was willing to let the Lord do whatever, I just did not know what it would take. But one thing I knew, something had to give.

Then one day I went to the church where I was serving as a youth pastor and minister of education and in my mind, I knew that I could go no further without a change. So, when I arrived I asked the secretary to hold all my calls and not let anyone in to see me. I locked my office door and began to pray. Soon I was laying on the ground with my face on the floor and all I could pray was, "Lord, you are either going to have to fill me or kill me." I know the Lord knew I was serious. I was desperate. I cried and pleaded with the Lord to fill me, because deep down I knew the answer to all my problems was a touch from Him. So many today are crying out for a touch, yet so few willing to surrender and then go through what I was about to go through. The Lord answered me alright, but it did not come in the way I expected. I was wanting a snap of God's fingers that instantly gave me great anointing and power, all the finances I wanted, and all the people around me to change so I could be successful. What the Lord did next would define me or destroy me based on how I responded. In a still small voice, yet a very clear voice that could not be mistaken, the Lord said, "Look at the finger you have been pointing at others. Realize the truth is that there are more fingers pointing back at you. YOU are the problem, not them. So, I am going to change you. This is where we will start. Remember the conversation you had with that Deacon the other day? Remember when he asked you if you had done something and you said you had but it was a lie to make you look good? You need to call him and admit your sin and ask his forgiveness." The Lord could have told me to go kill someone and I think that would have been easier for me to do. The Lord was asking me to humble myself and deal with a major problem I had in my younger days of ministry, lying to cover my inadequacies. I told the Lord that it was too hard, too humiliating. His response was, "I thought you surrendered everything and you were desperate for me to fill you?" He was right, I was so desperate I started thinking that one act of humiliation would be worth it. So, I slowly dialed the deacon's phone number and explained to him (without making any excuses) how I had lied to him and that I needed to ask his forgiveness. He was most gracious to me and told me that he sensed God was doing something good in my life and that he certainly forgave me. I had never felt more relieved in my life! I felt like the whole weight of the world had been lifted off of my shoulders. The joy I felt in that moment reminded me of David's prayer for the Lord to restore to him the joy of his salvation. I was on cloud nine experiencing an outpouring of God's grace because God gives grace to the humble and I had just humbled myself in a way I had never done before. I was literally experiencing the revival in my spirit I had desired and prayed for and sought for years! But it only lasted for about two minutes! Then the Lord spoke to me again. This time he asked me if I remembered lying to one of my close friends who attended our church. Again, I had lied to keep from looking bad. Of course, I remembered and the Lord told me that I needed to call him and make it right. Lord! One time was bad enough, but twice? The agony of whether or not I could humiliate myself again ripped through my soul. As I begged God again not to make me do it He again spoke clearly to me and said, "I thought you were serious about being filled. Are you, or aren't you? If you have truly surrendered and if you really want to be filled with my goodness, do it!" So again, I got the phone out and called my friend. This time it did not go nearly as well and I endured a loving rebuke. He was right so I humbly asked his forgiveness and then hung up the phone. Oh, the glory! The joy came back again! I felt like heaven on earth now that those two issues were resolved.

What I did not know at the time was that the Lord had brought me past the Altar of Sacrifice to the Bronze Laver, the place of cleansing. There the priests looked into the laver full of water that was made of bronze making the water just like a mirror. The symbolism was that the priest was to look in and see himself for who he really was and then see the need to be cleansed. He would then wash in the laver before going into the inner court. The laver represents cleansing from the world, the flesh, and demonic strongholds. It makes us face our sins of the lust of the eyes, the lust of the flesh, and the sinful pride of life. It was at this altar that one must pray Psalm 139:23-24 which says, *"Search me [thoroughly], O God, and know my heart! Try me and know my thoughts! And see if there is any wicked or hurtful way in me and lead me in the way everlasting."* I did not know at the time that the key to moving past the outer court was surrender and deliverance. Now I understand that one will remain in the outer court until one surrenders and until the Lord delivers him from evil. If we want to grow up, if we want revival, we are going to have to count the cost of holiness. We must seek His face and turn from our wicked ways. It will humble us, break us, and painfully kill our flesh, but the end result will be a joy previously unknown. Grace will begin to be poured out on you so tangibly that tears will flow easily just at the mention of His grace and love.

I wish I could say that after those two phone calls I was completely right with the Lord and right with everyone around me. I wasn't. As a matter of fact, for the next nine months, the Lord kept searching my heart and bringing into the light the sin I had kept in the darkness. I had to repent to my wife, my Pastor, my friends, my family, my landlady, people I had not seen in years, and some I did not care to ever see again. It was the most painful yet wonderful thing I had ever experienced up to that point in my life. The brokenness and cleansing at the Laver were great, but it may be the hardest step one takes in their spiritual journey, but it is absolutely necessary if we want a ceaseless flow of His Presence. Without the grace of God (mentioned earlier), this part of the journey would be impossible.

Here are a few examples of relationships I needed to right: Our worship leader at the time, who has since gone on to be with the Lord, was a wonderful man of God and a very wise man but his demeanor toward people tended to be on the harsh side. So people would come to me and complain and I would entertain their gossip and return some tidbits of my own, letting people know that I thought he could be annoying to say the least. I have since learned the destructive forces of gossip and strife, but at the time, people often came to me to vent. As soon as I entertained it and added more fuel to the fire, I sinned against God and against our worship leader. So the Lord convicted me of this and told me to go make it right. Yes, it was very humiliating, but by this time I learned that God would not relent until I had been obedient. So I went to him and righted the relationship and asked his forgiveness. He was most gracious and forgave me. Well, that was great except he was so annoying! I did not learn my lesson and within a week or two I had again listened to someone vent and I again passed on my opinion of him to that person. I was immediately convicted by the Holy Spirit and I knew immediately that I had to go back a second time to right the relationship. He was forgiving but not nearly as cordial. I was truly relieved. But, he was so annoying! Yes, I let someone know it for the third time! You guessed it. The Lord pricked my heart and told me to go back again! After several days of begging the Lord to not make me do it, He again asked me if I was surrendered and serious about my prayer to fill me or kill me. I said I was and went to him a third time. I do not even remember what he said, I just remember the utter humiliation I felt. This time I felt deep repentance for gossiping about him. My heart broke for him and I came to love and appreciate him more than ever from that point on. God is looking for true repentance and heart change at the Bronze Laver.

Another life changing act of repentance came a few years later. I had been called to another church to be their Youth Pastor and Minister of Education and I really loved the church and the people, but I was discontent as a Youth Pastor. I began asking God if he would allow me to become a Pastor. It was so strong on my heart to be a Pastor yet I was not getting any affirmation from the Lord. So one day I again got on my face before the Lord and asked Him why. As I lay there on my face before Him, I felt conviction of sin come over my whole body in a way I never had before nor have ever had since. The weight of the conviction was so powerful that I had to tell the Lord to please stop, I couldn't take the weight of my sin and I did not even know what the sin was. Eventually the conviction began to wane and the Lord spoke to me very clearly and directly and told me that the reason He had not given me freedom to pursue being a Pastor was because of the way I had treated the Pastors that I had served with. I had wonderful Pastors, men of God, loving servants of the Lord who loved me and my family. Yet I had often been quick to criticize, blame, and gossip about, let alone try to be submissive to. The Lord showed me that I could never lead as long as I treated the Lord's anointed how I had treated them. I could never lead if I could not follow. It definitely broke me and I immediately began making contact with them and repenting before them and asking their forgiveness. The Lord showed me that I had a spirit like Absalom in me that undermined my pastors and created division in the body. I even once tried to start my own church and in my heart I was thinking who from my church I could take with me. I would run into the Absalom spirit in others later in my ministry and I learned how to deal with it because I had to deal with it in me first. I could share many more humiliating experiences but hopefully you get the point.

At the laver of deliverance, one will have to deal with the flesh as I did. One will also have to deal with overcoming worldliness. There is only one thing that overcomes the world, our faith. My financial discontent was finally broken during that time in my life when I told the Lord that I would be OK living in a tent with no money if that is what it took to serve Him and honor Him. I would trust Him by faith. About ten years after those long nine months, the Lord showed me the demonic strongholds and mindsets that had me bound as well and how to be delivered from them. That is also another book in itself. The Lord delivered me from pride, rejection, legalism, religion, fear of man, and several other areas of sin that had a "strong hold" on me. When I closed the doors to those root issues in my life that I had opened to the enemy, I again soared to new heights in the Spirit. So, my experience of moving from the outer court to the inner court was a long one but well worth it. Hopefully for you it will be much shorter. We all must go through it, though. Yes, it will be extremely humbling but it will also be extremely life changing. Going into the inner court and its furnishings began a whole new chapter in my life that still amazes me today. The next chapter will be about how to enter into that inner court. Let me finish this teaching on the outer court with this: How hungry are you? Are you willing to ask the Lord to search you and know you and show you everything that is keeping you from moving forward spiritually? Will you obey when He shows you how to deal with it? Are you crying out for Him to fill you or kill you? Have you surrendered all? Do you want revival so desperately that you are willing to follow 2 Chronicles 7:14 that says we must humble ourselves and pray and turn from our wicked ways? So many of us desire revival but do not want the deep cleansing first. That is what the outer court is all about. I am sure that if I had not allowed the

Lord to search my heart and then persevered the cleansing, I would have become so frustrated with ministry that I would have left my calling. I am so glad he gave me grace to humble myself and pray, to seek His face, and to turn from my wicked ways. Because now He is hearing me from heaven, He has forgiven my sin, and He is bringing healing and restoration to me and my ministry and He has restored to me the joy of my salvation. You can trust that there will be days when you just cannot humble yourself any further but you will ask for grace, His desire and power to accomplish His will, and He will give it to you and you will have power to endure the fire.

One more interesting truth about the outer court. It had no roof, no covering. It was governed by natural circumstances and situations. It was rained on as well as received sunlight. There was night times and cold times. It was lit by the sun. This is obvious as it corresponds to most Christians lives. Most Christians live what I call "roller coaster" Christianity. They are up and down, happy and sad, encouraged then discouraged, on and off, tossed to and fro, and lack the necessary covering that will stabilize their walk. When the church understands that they can surrender and be delivered, they will move into the inner court, a place that is not only covered, but is lit by the candlestick, the Holy Spirit. Then after they move into the Holy of Holies, it is not only covered, but will be lit by the glory of God!

Chapter 5: Understanding the Priestly
(The Inner Court)

At the edge of the outer court stood an entrance. It was the entrance to the Holy Place or the inner court. When one moves out of the outer court through surrender and deliverance, one moves into a whole new place in their walk with the Lord. The entrance into the next stage of spiritual maturity is accessed by faith and grace, just as the entrance to the outer court was. Upon entering through the door of the inner court the first piece of furniture the High Priest encountered was the candlestick. It represents the fullness of the Holy Spirit. The seven candles represented the seven spirits found in Isaiah 11:2. He is the Spirit, the Spirit of Wisdom, the Spirit of Understanding, the Spirit of Counsel, the Spirit of Might, the Spirit of Knowledge, and the Spirit of the Reverential Fear of the Lord. The number seven represents fullness or completion or perfection so we know the seven candles represent the fullness of the Holy Spirit.

Receiving the fullness of the Holy Spirit or the baptism of the Holy Spirit can happen at any time to a Christian. One does not have to be surrendered or delivered to experience Him. This is not a religious pattern or legalistic pattern, it is a principle of growth. The reason that the candlestick is placed where it is in the tabernacle is because if one is filled with the power of God but is unsubmitted or unholy or undelivered, that person could be in for a big fall. Fruit of the Spirit is just as important as the gifts of the Spirit if not more so. We do not tell a tree by its power, we tell a tree by its fruit.

There are already many books out there on how to receive the baptism. My goal is just to tell you that it is a necessary part of growth that takes us into the Holy of Holies and into a ceaseless flow of oil. When one receives the baptism of the Spirit by faith one's spiritual life gets turned upside down. At least it did for me. In one great move of the Spirit upon my life I had the operations of the Holy Spirit working powerfully in my life. I preached with power, I laid hands on the sick and many recovered, I cast out demons in Jesus name and people were absolutely set free and transformed, I had Holy Spirit illumination when I studied the Word, I had power to walk in holiness. The anointing of the Holy Spirit on a believer's life will be one major key to a lifetime of effective ministry, holiness, and revelation.

Every priest had to be anointed (see Ex. 40:15). Each of us must rely on the anointing if we are to walk in supernatural ministry. What we do not realize is that same anointing propels us forward in our relationship with the Father. No priest ever went into the Holy of Holies without being anointed with oil. Remember, the anointing is the anointing of the *Holy* Spirit. We are definitely miraculously empowered for ministry, but also for entrance into the Holy of Holies. The altar of surrender and deliverance bring a great deal of holiness, but the anointing takes us to a new realm of inner holiness. The anointing sets us up for a baptism of fire, true inner purification that results in a baptism of fire for a deeper power than we have ever known.

Many have felt that the baptism of the Holy Spirit is the end or the Promised Land of Christianity. No, the candlestick is only half way to the Holy of Holies and the Manifest Presence of God. Whole denominations were birthed as a result of the baptism, but we must not camp there! Is it important? Absolutely! But it is just a means to the ends of His covenant promises, His Shekinah Glory, and the ceaseless flow of oil. We should seek the gifts, the anointing, and power for miraculous ministry, but we should not seek His hand more than His face. If my people, who are called by my Name, will humble themselves and pray, and seek my *FACE*, then I will hear from heaven, I will forgive their sins, and I will heal their land! Do you want national revival? Then receive the baptism of the Holy

Spirit and then keep pressing on! Do not stop there! You must be empowered by the anointing to walk through the next sections of the tabernacle. There is no deep revelation without the anointing (the Bread of the Presence) nor any intense prayer and intercession (Altar of Incense) without the baptism, and so on. Eagerly desire the baptism, but more so desire HIM!

The next piece of furniture is the Bread of the Presence. It consisted of twelve loaves of bread, one for each tribe of Israel. It was also called the Bread of the Presence because it represents Jesus, the Bread of Life. We should desire His Presence more than anything else in life. We should desire Him more than miracles, power, church growth, or even salvations. If we have His Presence, we will have all of those things! The cool thing is that after my Holy Spirit baptism, I began experiencing God in wonderful new ways. The Bread of the Presence also represents revelation, as the manna of heaven did. It represents spiritual sustenance. Man cannot live by bread alone, but by every word that proceeds from the mouth of the Lord. In the inner court God's Word will become alive!

As our church went to the Bread of the Presence, the Lord began to show us great and unsearchable things we did not know. It was at this stage that the Lord gave me the revelation of the ceaseless flow of oil. Our new church had experienced wonderful manifestations of power and gifts, and many received the gift of praying in tongues. But this revelation of Jesus was phenomenal. The Lord showed us that it is the glory of God to conceal a matter but it was the glory of kings to seek it out. We became kings that desperately sought out the spiritual mysteries of God (see Matthew 13:11, 1 Corinthians 4:1). The twelve loaves also symbolize divine government. The number twelve in Scripture is very important and pertains often to government. It was here that the Lord began to reveal to us divine order and church government. We began the transition to a five-fold government as taught in Ephesians 4:10-14. It has been a great joy to walk in the Bread of the Presence. It has not been without heartache, though. It seems like our church would start to grow and be blessed, and the Lord would give us another step of obedience or order and some would not submit. It was like the story of Gideon. Some left because they feared or were not comfortable with what the Lord was doing and saying. Others left because they did not agree to "drink with the hand" (the hand often in Scripture represents a fivefold government). The road to the Holy of Holies gets narrower and narrower with each piece of furniture. The great promise is for the overcomers as seen in the Book of Revelation in chapters two and three. Even though the road gets narrower, the presence of the Lord becomes more wonderful, more powerful, and more tangible with each step toward the Holy of Holies!

What I thought would be the most wonderful part of the journey through the tabernacle pattern was the Altar of Incense. It stood right at the entrance to the Holy of Holies. The burning incense going up to the Father symbolizes intense worship and intense prayer. Since we were a church that believed firmly in prayer and in worship, we felt like this stage was going to be a breeze. We set aside Monday nights to be a night of intense prayer and worship. I remember being so excited about the first night because I knew that we were so close to the Holy of Holies, just a whisper away. At least that is what I thought. The first night did not turn out anything like I envisioned. I sat in the back row for over an hour as we tried to break through to the Lord's presence in worship. I came under some of the most intense spiritual warfare I have ever been attacked by. The enemy was trying to stop us at this stage. Although I eventually broke through that night, that warfare would set the stage for the Altar of Incense.

As we continued to meet every week to pray and worship (we often fasted as well for various lengths of time), it became obvious that the attacks were not going to stop. So I began to further study the Altar of Incense and realized that the ingredients that made up the incense had to be crushed into very fine powder and then it was burned! The stage of the Altar of Incense became some of the most difficult years of my life. The Lord definitely crushed us and sent us through the fire. Yet we kept praying and worshipping and being faithful. Without God's grace to encourage us during those days, we would not have survived. One day the Lord really encouraged me by showing me again that the prayers that we had been praying were being stored in heaven and would be answered. What we were doing was not in vain. He showed me that the stage of the Altar of Incense would last as long as it needed to until we all became a sweet-smelling aroma to the Lord! He showed me that we had endured a very difficult shaking so that all that could be shaken would be shaken. Then all that would be left was for us to receive the Kingdom! WOW! That made it all worth it.

Yet there was yet another place to go, into the very Holy of Holies. What we did not plan on was the revelation of the veil (a veil covered the Holy of Holies but was torn from top to bottom through the death of Jesus) of our hearts had to be torn, our hearts needed to be circumcised in order to enter in. When God says spotless bride, He means it! We have given the Lord complete permission to crush us, refine us in the fire, and circumcise us until there is only Jesus left in us! I have to admit that during those days God searched way deep into our hearts and showed us things that we did not know were hidden there. He showed us that they were hidden but given the right circumstances, the dark places would come out and manifest and possibly ruin us or our ministries. We have not been in a hurry to get into the Holy of Holies because we know that even when the Israelites crossed into the Promised Land the hidden sin in Achan's heart was made manifest and cost him his life, the life of his family, and the life of several Hebrew warriors. I am not saying not to take this journey, we must if we want to see end times revival and mega grace. I am saying that it will cost you everything. Some of the leaders in our church were even lost along the way. But the journey into the Holy of Holies, His covenant intimacy and manifestations, await those who are completely surrendered and willing to pay the price.

The Holy of Holies? What does it take to enter in? A passion for Him like no other. Every other passion must go. What do we receive? Love. Another triad that represents the three courts is faith, hope, and love. Entering into the Holy of Holies is entering into the very love of God in us and through us. It represents the most intimate relationship with Jesus that we could long for. Also, in the Most Holy Place, every promise becomes yes and amen in Christ! We will walk in covenant manifestations. When joined with the kingly anointing, there will be a flow of the Holy Spirit as the world has never seen. How will we ever see promises such as that of Ezekiel 39 come to pass? How can we see such divine intervention that an attack on Israel will result in destruction of the enemy so great it will not be completely cleaned up for seven years? Only through intercessors who stand in the gap and give God no rest until there is peace in Jerusalem, but those intercessors will need mega grace to have that prayer answered. How will we ever see nations born in a day? Only with grace, grace. Only with a ceaseless flow of oil. Do you long for an end times revival and harvest? Walk the journey through the tabernacle and watch the Lord bring you into covenant manifestations reserved for these last days!

The High Priest longed for the Holy of Holies. So should we. We as priests, had the veil rent in two at the cross and now have open access to Him. Yet we must still take the journey from the door of the tabernacle through the outer court with the Altar of Sacrifice and the cleansing Laver to the inner court with its Candlestick, Table of Showbread and its Altar of Incense. We must do it with the same fear of the Lord that the High Priest had. Only then can we enter into the Holy of Holies, under the shelter of His wings, into His very manifest presence. We have fallen short of His glory, this high calling to go into the Holy of Holies, because some stopped along the way and never progressed any further. We must be like Moses who saw the power of God but was not content until he saw the glory of God. In the last days, the Lord is going to restore the Tabernacle of David. That tabernacle consisted only of the Holy of Holies. Zechariah 13:8 says that in the last days two thirds of the land or Israel will be cut off while the remaining third will be refined in the fire. In other words, those not entering in to covenant relationship with the Lord are in danger of being taken out in the last great shaking. They are saved and going to heaven but falling short of their destinies.

The priestly function of the believer is very important because the journey to intimacy with Jesus should be our priority in life. Therefore, we must be priests that are absolutely head over heels in love with our Savior. We must take the journey of love, the tabernacle pattern to the Presence of God. When we are progressing faithfully, zealously, and consistently toward the Holy of Holies, the olive tree representing our priestly role will pour out its oil.

Chapter 6: Understanding the Kingly
(The Kingly Anointing)

One night at church we were talking about how wonderful the presence of the Lord had been in our church. One of our members, Brenda, said that she knew when she noticed a shift in our church. She knew that we had founded our church on the priestly, the desire to grow in intimacy with the Lord. We had stressed it from day one. The difference, though, she said came after a message on binding and loosing. We had begun combining the kingly with the priestly. She was right! The combination of the kingly and priestly revved up the engine of the ceaseless flow of the Holy Spirit. You, too, will experience the flow as you walk in the kingly and priestly. Some churches emphasize the priestly, some the kingly, but we must walk in both. Today we see miracle after miracle as we get in the presence and then hear and then decree and move in power and authority. One morning I was going to preach and right as I was sitting down I heard the Lord say, "And He healed them all." As a priest, I knew the voice of the Lord. So, when it came time to preach, I knew I had to cast aside my prepared message. I just stood up and said that today He was going to heal them all! As a king, I decreed what I heard, shared some truths about how we have full access to healing, then we prayed for the sick. Every single person was healed. Blind eyes were opened, tumors left bodies, joint pain disappeared, and on and on. One man had tumors covering both arms. As I prayed for him I put my hands on his arms and said, "Come Holy Spirit. Be healed in Jesus name!" But I never had to ask him how he felt because the tumors dissolved under my hands. Every tumor was gone instantly! Another time I was preaching in Pakistan in front of thousands and I told that testimony of the man whose tumors on his arms all disappeared. After I shared that testimony, a famous Muslim man walked up on stage and interrupted the message. I had to completely stop preaching as the man began talking to my interpreter. I was then told that this famous Muslim man also had tumors all over both of his arms and wanted to be healed! What do you do when you have thousands watching to see what God does? You believe it is not by might, not by power, but by my Spirit says the Lord! So, one word of knowledge that led to a miracle was now opening the door for another miracle. Sure enough, I just put my hand on his arm and said come Holy Spirit be healed in Jesus name and the arm became completely clear of tumors and then we did the same for the other arm. Being a priest and a king changes lives! That famous Muslim man now goes around Pakistan telling the testimony of how He was healed by Jesus!!It is the normal Christian life. We need to understand the kingly anointing as well as the priestly.

The other olive tree was another son of oil, Zerubbabel. He was the prince or governor of Judah. He represents the Kingdom or the rule and reign of God, His government, divine order, authority, power, and dominion. We must understand that Jesus told us to seek first the Kingdom (Kingly role) and His righteousness (Priestly role). Peter tells us that we are to be a royal priesthood. John tells us in the book of Revelation that we are a kingdom of priests. These two anointings must go together. This tells us that the Kingly role is also absolutely essential just as the priestly role is. We must have a Kingdom mentality. When we as individuals and as churches begin walking in this Kingly anointing as well as fall head over heels in love with Jesus, the oil will pour out into a power unseen in human history. Let's take a closer look at the Kingly anointing of the believer.

First of all, the church has been a mess for many years because it has not understood divine government or divine order. When the Israelites were encamped according to their tribes and Balaam came to curse them, he could not (Numbers 24:2). Israel was in divine order. The twelve tribes were encamped according to tribe with the tabernacle and the ark of the covenant right in the center of the camp. That is a picture of divine government and the priestly function at work. Not only could Balaam not curse Israel, he also had to bless them. We have heard a lot of talk about the gates of hell not prevailing against the church and Christians being the head and not the tail, yet why is it that the enemy has the church on the ropes most of the time? It is because we do not understand divine order in the churches. Divine order or the kingly anointing consists of at least the following parts:

Church government: The church has had the idea that if the congregation can vote a Pastor in, they can vote him out. That is tragic. Some churches have a board of deacons or directors that run the church. Other churches are set up to have church councils or committees propose items at business meetings, to be voted on by the whole church, to make the decisions of the church. Spiritual maturity levels do not matter, anyone can give their "two-cents worth" and can link arms with enough other members and pass any item of business they want. This is tragic and is found nowhere in Scripture. Every church should be led by apostles, prophets, evangelists, pastors, and teachers. These are the "headship" gifts given as Jesus ascended (Ephesians 4:7-11). The congregation submits to these elders. The congregation, of course, can and should give wise counsel to the leaders for them to consider, but the five-fold leaders make the final decisions. Without them leading the church, there will never be maturity in the body, there will never be perfection. It is the responsibility of the five-fold to bring the body to perfection and fullness (Ephesians 4:7-16). Why? Because without being clean and perfect, the High Priest could not enter the Holy of Holies! The ten days leading up to the Day of Atonement were days of repentance and brokenness. It is no different for us. Without holiness, purity, and brokenness, no one will see the Lord. The church is far from being spotless and mature or perfect. The church is being tossed by winds of doctrine and is not growing up.

We also need the five-fold functioning to properly equip and cleanse the body. This is why the kingly and priestly roles work hand in hand. The priest cannot enter in the Holy of Holies without the five-fold ministry in operation. Without entering the Holy of Holies, the power and glory will be limited. Why has this not been working? Because the five-fold is busy (if there even is a five-fold in operation, which is very rare) pleasing a bunch of followers in order to keep their jobs! We also have this idea that the Pastor is the leader of the church. No! He is just one of the five-fold working together in unity to lead the church. God never intended for one man to be everything to everybody. Even Moses found that out the hard way. God gave Moses leaders over thousands, hundreds, fifties, and tens. That is a five-fold ministry! There may be a "point-man" in the church, but no one can do it all. How much power and anointing will be available if these five offices work together to lead the church with the congregation submitting to their loving leadership. This divine government must be in place. Then when the world tries to curse the church it will end up blessing it! The gates of hell will not prevail against such a church.

The Old Testament pattern (which is a type and shadow of the New) was seen in the books of Kings and Chronicles. A King established his rulership (by being anointed by the prophet as God's man and by being recognized by the people), set up his government (king, prophet, commander of armies, priests, scribes – cf. apostles, prophets, evangelists, pastors, teachers), then expanded his rule. Secondly, the king established his rule over his subjects with benevolence, then expanded his rule and relations with the people. Thirdly, the king established his rule over the land and resources, then protected them with strongholds, then expanded his territory through warfare. Whole books could be written on this subject alone. For now, suffice it to say that churches need to rethink their church government from a Biblical divine order perspective.

Divine order: The prophet declared in Isaiah 40:3-5 that the Lord would manifest Himself to the Jews only when every valley was filled in, every mountain was removed, every crooked road was made straight, and all the potholes were filled in. Only then was the road worthy of a King traveling on it. Only then would there be a manifestation of His glory! This, of course, is the passage that John the Baptist quoted during his ministry (Luke 3:4-5). We, too, have only one way to prepare the way of the Lord. The whole Body of Christ, churches, families and we as individuals must get our lives in order. We must get our marriages in divine order where the husbands lovingly lead and sacrifice for their wives and children and wives give wonderful counsel to their husbands yet lovingly submit to his role and leadership. Children stay under the covering of their parents with honor and respect, employees and employers have their spiritual and marketplace anointings in order, and even our finances are in line with the Word of God, etc. We must be in order physically (we are eating right and exercising properly), and our souls are in order (our mind, will and emotions are all submitted to our spirit). And of course, the church is in order and in submission to the fivefold government and eldership of the church. Many sermons could be preached about all of these areas of our lives.

Our church fasted and prayed for the Lord to show us how to get our church and personal lives in order. These were some of our hardest days as God was faithful to show us how far we had allowed ourselves to get out of order. Many relationships were restored, others left the church rather than get in order. Many personal issues of sin were brought to the surface, many were cleansed, others left rather than deal with the sin issues. With every season of the Lord moving us into divine order (He did not do it all at once), we went from one level of glory to the next! Each time we allowed Him to search deeper into our hearts, He obliged! The blessings of His presence that resulted were very worth it, though. Divine order will be opposed by the religious and the self-righteous but is essential if we are to see the Lord walk down that path we have prepared in the desert. The good news is that Zechariah 4 says that these obstacles, these mountains, will be made into a plain with shouts of grace, grace to it. There will be a double portion of grace for all who are willing to get into divine order! It is the role of church government (the plumb line will be in the hands of Zerubbabel) to lead a church to get their lives and their church in order (see Ephesians 4:11-15).

Authority: When a King made a decree, it was carried out and not even the King could change his mind, as we see in the story of Daniel and the lion's den (Daniel 6). We are kings and when we get a Word from the King of kings we are to declare it and decree it (see Psalm 2:7, Job 22:28). We do not need to ask for these things, we are to use our authority to command these things into being. If it has been loosed in heaven, we can loose it here (Matthew 16:19). God is just waiting for someone to agree with heaven. For example, we know by the Word of God that it is God's will for us to be sanctified (1 Thessalonians 4:3). So why ask for it? We are to command it! We should say, "Sanctification, come in Jesus Name!" That is how the Lord's Prayer teaches us to pray (Matthew 6:9-13). There are seven imperative verbs in that prayer. It should read, "Kingdom, come!" "Will, be done!" These are not options, these are imperative commands that Jesus Himself told us we are to command. "Daily bread, come!" Deliverance from evil, come!" "Name of God, be hallowed!" Since we know what God wants for His Kingdom, we need to use our Kingly authority and begin making faith declarations and loose the Kingdom on earth as it is in heaven. "Glory of God, come! Grace, come! Salvations, come! Love, come! Faith, come! Brokenness and humility, come! Revival, come! Miracles, signs, and wonders, come! Surrender, come! Sickness, be bound!" If we are not sure what the will of God is pertaining to a specific situation, we are to ask, seek, and knock until the Lord reveals His will for the situation. Once He does, we can command His will to be done. "Will, be done in Jesus Name!" For example, if one is praying about selling their house and the Lord reveals to them that they are to sell it, that one should then make the command, "House, be sold in Jesus Name! Buyer, come in Jesus Name!" These are all governmental, Kingly decrees we can make as Kings when we have received clear direction from the King of kings.

In Isaiah 45:11 God commands His children to "Command ye Me!" If we are Kings, and we are, we must act like Kings.

One of the greatest principles in all of Scripture has been used for getting people saved and then it is forgotten. Romans 10:9-10 tells us that we need to believe in our heart and confess with our mouths. This same principle goes for the rest of our spiritual lives as well. What are we believing God for and confessing with our mouth, what governmental decrees are we making? These are the keys (authority) of the Kingdom that we must use. We must use these keys to enforce the victory that was won at Calvary. We cannot let the enemy lift up his head against the victory of the cross. We must crush every work of the enemy that implies the cross of Christ was devoid of power. We are to use our authority to destroy the works of the enemy, especially when we are always led in triumph and the enemy has been soundly defeated. As enforcers of the victory, we have great authority. It was authority and power that was given to the apostles and is given to us. We must use it and take our place as enforcers of the Kingdom mandate on earth.

Dominion: Many are waiting for the return of Christ. We are looking at the signs of the times and we are trying to figure out when it will be and what it will look like. We too often overlook a very important sign of the times that must take place before He returns. It is found in Acts 3:21 and it says that there will be no return of the Lord until the restitution or restoration of all things. We should see the church operate today in the dominion it had in the Garden. All of creation groans for this manifestation to take place (Romans 8:20-22). It will not take place until the sons of God are made manifest (Romans 8:18-22). We have authority over the animals, the land, the winds, the waves, the climates and the storms just as Jesus did. We also have dominion over the enemy. Jesus restored our dominion by returning to us the keys of the Kingdom. The church today has been deceived into powerlessness. When we walk in this dominion, then we can look for the return of the Lord. For today, let us walk in dominion and we will see the church boom and the enemy defeated as the church takes back the ground the enemy has stolen.

Kingdom living or living as a citizen of heaven: We need to understand the culture of heaven, the economy of heaven, the laws of heaven, the riches of heaven, the glory of heaven, everything about heaven. That culture is then to be released from heaven to earth, thy Kingdom come on earth as it is in heaven. Everything in heaven is accessible to us here as citizens of heaven! Then we need to learn how a kingdom citizen lives. Jesus never taught the Gospel of the Church, He taught the Gospel of the Kingdom. His first message was that the Kingdom of heaven was at hand! Because we know so little about Kingdom living, we see only a small trickle of oil. When we understand the divine government of the Kingdom, we will leap forward in our faith and love for the Lord! Also, we will leap forward in appropriating the benefits of the Kingdom. We need to understand that He is King and we carry out the task of expanding His Kingdom by exemplifying it to the world and being ambassadors of the Kingdom.

Another forgotten principle of the Kingdom is that we are seated in the heavenlies with Christ! Think about that! We are, by grace, seated as a part of the council of elders that make the decisions for our sphere of authority. That sphere of authority could be dominion over our households, our neighborhoods, whole cities, states, or nations! We are seated in the place of authority just like the Supreme Court of the United States. They did not get voted in, they did not buy their way in, they were appointed by the President. In the same way, we found favor with the King and He appointed us or seated us in the heavenlies to rule and reign with Jesus Christ Himself! What are you loosing over your region? What are you binding? If you are not taking your seat of authority who is? The enemy will gladly take your authority and loose his evil upon your community or family if you allow him to. We need to get in our seats of authority and begin to declare and decree His will over our region. This is what kings do. We have been appointed for such a time as this to call forth His will over our families and communities and our churches. It is there we assign angels to fight, to gather, and to minister. It is there we bind the works of the enemy. It is there we invite heaven to earth. God Himself has seated us as joint heirs with Christ, to rule and to reign from our seats in the heavenlies!

Kings go to war and take new territory: The kings of the Old Testament are again shadows of the New. They went to war. It was the glory of their Kingdom to take new territory. If their land was expanding, wow s their glory, their name, and their reputation. If they were being defeated, so was there legacy. The Caesars of Rome greatly expanded the Roman Empire and are thus greatly remembered today. As kings, we, too, must go to war and take new territory. Who are we fighting for? What is our target? Kings did not haphazardly go to war, they strategized and planned and put the right soldiers and leaders in the right place. Most churches do not know what territory they are called to take nor is their church organized to take that territory. Most churches tell their people to just go and make disciples and then come back and testify when a life is transformed. Do you ever wonder why there are so few testimonies? Yes, we are to go and make disciples but that is like telling a soldier to go fight and win their own personal war wherever they are. A band of soldiers may be as small as two or three but if they do not have vision, strategy, direction and equipping, they will fail. In order to see a ceaseless flow of oil, we must organize to fight and win. Otherwise the oil will be wasted. One can put a thousand to flight, but two will put ten thousand to flight. What will happen if we have more than two, a Spirit led battle plan, and a ceaseless flow of oil? Whole cities and nations will be taken for the Kingdom! Kings go to war!

Who do kings fight? Our battle is not against flesh and blood but against spiritual forces in dark places. While Christians are busy fighting against each other, the enemy strategically takes new territory. We were never meant to fight one another! We must fight against the enemy. We had many battles against spiritual forces in our church. We fought Jezebel spirits, spirits of religion, Absalom spirits, antichrist spirits, lawlessness, witchcraft, spirits of immorality, baal, mammon, and the list goes on. We did not fight the people, we fought the spirits that were opposing what the Lord was doing in our midst. Some battles were fierce and we did not always know what we were doing, but the Lord was faithful to show us how to fight along the way. When we got weary in the battle, the enemy knew it and tried to take advantage. So, we learned to ask for more grace and more revelation as to how to keep fighting. We fought with prayer and fasting, we fought with the Word, and we fought with love. Sometimes we just blew it and hurt feelings along the way. We did not get it perfect all the time but we kept fighting for the Kingdom to be made manifest in our church and our community. If you want a ceaseless flow of oil, you are going to have to fight for it. Our fight did not last just one round. It went many rounds and is still not over. The fight has lasted for years. Hopefully our fight is clearing a path so your fight will not be as difficult, but all who are to be kings will fight. When a battle is won, that territory is then claimed for the Kingdom of Light. We must keep fighting until the Light overtakes the darkness!

Kings dispossess and destroy the works of the enemy: Many kings of Judah not only went to war and were victorious, but they had to rebuild the cities and the desolate places that their enemies had destroyed. In order to rebuild a city, a king had to tear down the altars to foreign gods, tear down the weak foundations of the city, and change the mindsets of the inhabitants of the city. Then he could rebuild the city according to his kingdom agenda. We live in a day where the foundations of cities and nations are built upon the sand of the world and they must be overtaken and rebuilt. Cities back then were often built on mounds or hills for their own protection. We are to change cities because we are to be like a city on a hill, one that is protected, but also one that shines the light of the Kingdom of God for other cities to see.

Saul was anointed to dispossess the Philistine garrison that had taken possession of God's hill (see 1 Sam. 10:5). Even Jesus came to destroy the works of the enemy. We are not kings if we are not fighting to loose the Kingdom of Light and destroy the deeds of darkness. What hills has the enemy taken in your community? Who is at the top of the hill, the place of strength and authority? Who is the President or governor or mayor or politician who is at the top of the hill? Is it possessed by a God ordained and anointed person or is it occupied by the enemy? What about your local school board or Little League? Who are the top influencers in your marketplace? Who sets the entertainment agenda for your city? Kings are called to dispossess the enemy and install their officers and soldiers into those places of influence. We will not see our nation change with just revival. We must use the outpouring to destroy the works of the enemy, to displace and replace those Philistines that are on God's hill. After dispossessing the enemy, we also have to destroy the mindset that was loosed through that leader. Did that leader embrace homosexual unions and give compelling arguments for it? That leader must be dispossessed and that mindset must be challenged, destroyed, and replaced using wisdom, truth, and revelation under the anointing and that issue will be defeated and destroyed. He who is on top of the hill sets the agenda for the kingdom or the community. Every believer fits on at least one cultural hill and must fight to climb that hill alone or with others that the Lord has anointed to do so. Kings do not sit back and watch their enemies set the agenda for their culture. We must see this in this hour. Do we not remember that the anti-christ will attempt to do this? Why will he be so opposed to Christians? Because they are the only ones that can occupy and set up God's Kingdom agenda in cities and nations. It will be either rule or be ruled! **Forget the separation of church and state**, the church must be the salt and light of the state. If we are not, the state will be ruled by darkness and the church will be forced to live in the darkness and the church's influence will be minimal. Kings, rise up!

Kings control the wealth: Kings used the resources they had to bring honor and glory to their Kingdom. Finances flowed in from conquered foes. Wealth also went to lift the standard of living for those in the Kingdom. It would be a dishonor to see citizens that were poor. The French revolution came about because the kings were evil and selfish, keeping the prosperity for themselves and allowing the peasants to go hungry. With all the verses in Scripture that describe the riches and the resources as God's, do we still think He does not want us to have these resources as tools to expand His Kingdom? Yes, some riches have been received and abused. That is why we need to be priests as well as kings, those that do not love money but love Jesus and understand that money is used to win friends for the Kingdom of God. The Queen of Sheba recognized the greatness of Solomon's kingdom when she saw its extravagance. Why is the church just as bad off as the world? Because we have been unfaithful with the money. Great kings used their money for the expansion of their kingdom and for the benevolence of its citizens. Let's be kings in the area of finances. When we understand the kingly and priestly concerning finances, we will see a ceaseless flow of finances as well!

Kings advance culture: As a kid I used to enjoy looking at pictures of the "wonders of the world." Things like the pyramids of Egypt, the hanging gardens of Babylon, the Pharos of Alexandria. These were usually tributes to the king or to the king's gods. Cultures nowadays are advancing at incredible speed which was prophesied by Daniel (Daniel 12:4). The internet, global television, satellite televisions, radios, and telephones connect the world in ways that have shrunk the already small world. Ask people in China who their favorite actor is and you might hear the answer "George Clooney." Ask people in India where they bought their last book and they might answer "From Great Britain on E-bay." Ask someone from Australia where they received their college degree and they may tell you they took online courses from Canada. Kings must recognize the incredible power available to them to change the world through the kingdom of culture. Movies and television shows shape mindsets, news sites and magazines give the information they want to give that promotes their agenda. Christians should not have as their goal to boycott Hollywood, their goal should be to take over Hollywood and reshape the culture! Kings know how to place people with gifts in strategic places to change the mindsets of cities and nations. They can expose lies and promote truth. He who wins the culture war wins the people.

Kings advance their spiritual values: The great kings of Scripture promoted obedience to the Law of God. The bad kings led the people away from the Lord to seek false gods. What spiritual advancement are we promoting? Probably most of us are not promoting false gods, but are we truly promoting spiritual growth and deep Kingdom advancement? A seldom quoted but very important passage of Scripture is found in Hebrews 6:1-3. It says that we are to move past elementary teachings and go on to perfection or maturity. The old Catholic church used to keep its people in the dark spiritually by not allowing them to read the Bible for themselves. Unfortunately, today's body of Christ is almost as ignorant because we keep teaching on salvation, faith, laying on of hands, end times, and etc. Those teachings are vital and extremely important and we should never neglect them. But they are elementary school. Go to a Christian bookstore and browse the Christian Living section and see if there is anything new, anything that grows a believer to perfection. Most books I see say the same thing. Why is that? It is not because we have bad authors, it is because that is what is selling because that is where the body is spiritually, way back in elementary school. Where are the kings that will advance the Kingdom violently by daring to move past elementary teachings and therefore build a strong body. We should be a body that is no longer tossed to and fro by every wind of doctrine, and we should be a people that fights against stagnation. We should listen and seek the Lord. We will be amazed at our growth when we do. Jeremiah said that the Lord will show us great and unsearchable things that we do not know! I long for those revelations from the Lord because I do not know it all nor does anyone I know have all the revelation. The Lord will continue to give understanding of His Word if we choose to move past elementary teachings.

Kings are servants: The greatest kings in Scripture had the glory of God as their focus and not their own personal glory. The greatest kings in Scripture served the people of their kingdom in order to bless them and make the whole kingdom great. Jesus is the greatest King and came as a servant. When the disciples started to get the revelation about their kingship and apostleship and authority, they began to argue about who was the greatest. Jesus clearly taught them that the greatest among them was the one that served the others. During a deacon ordination at a church I served we ordained some wonderful men. Those already ordained were to lay hands on the new deacons and whisper a word of encouragement to them. As I approached one of the men the Lord spoke to me about what to say. The Lord told me to tell him that he was called to be a man that did not focus on the politics of the church nor gain a name for himself, but that he was to out serve all the rest of the deacons and that would please the Lord. Later that new deacon told me that was the word that stood out to him and that would be his goal as a deacon or servant of the Lord. The world sees the king at the top of the leadership pyramid. The Lord sees the king at the bottom of the leadership pyramid, the one undergirding the rest of the citizens of the kingdom. Want oil? Be a servant king!

Kings unite! A king that joined forces with another king or with several kings was much stronger than by himself. One will put a thousand to flight, two will put ten thousand to flight. Jesus prayed that we be as one. Unity in the body of Christ is hard enough to find in churches let alone between churches. I attended a "church growth" meeting one time where the consultant asked us who are main competition was. I was thinking that our competition was all the nearby recreational facilities that were keeping people from church. Instead, he wanted to know what other churches were in the area, as they were our competition. Unfortunately, that is the mindset of many Christians, Pastors, and leaders. We are at the ready to steal sheep from other sheepfolds if necessary to build our house. We need to join forces! We need Pastors and elders and leaders to work together to do Kingdom business. The book of Haggai says that because we are building our own houses, the Lord has withheld blessing over our communities:

"You look for much, but behold, it comes to little; when you bring it home, I blow it away. Why?" declares the LORD of hosts, "Because of My house which lies desolate, while each of you runs to his own house. 10 "Therefore, because of you the sky has withheld its dew and the earth has withheld its produce. 11 "I called for a drought on the land, on the mountains, on the grain, on the new wine, on the oil, on what the ground produces, on men, on cattle, and on all the labor of your hands." (Haggai 1:9-11)

The United States has treaties with many nations for the sake of their strength and protection and to have someone to stand with them. How much more so do we, in the body of Christ, need to stand with one another and stand together as churches to destroy the works of the enemy. Kings do not compete with one another, that weakens both armies, instead they join together to form a massive coalition against the enemy!

Obviously, there is much more that can be said about each of the Kingly and priestly functions. We could talk of Elijah who called fire down from heaven after repairing the altar (priestly role) with twelve stones (twelve is the number of divine government or of the kingly role). We could talk more about Melchizadek who was a priest and a king. We could talk of Samuel who was a priest and the governing official of Israel. We could talk of the disastrous decision Israel made to separate the kingly and priestly by asking for a king. The bottom line, however, is that because we are not walking as Kings and priests, the oil is not flowing. When will we fall in love with Jesus? When will we allow the Holy Spirit to search us and know us and reveal anything and everything that is out of divine order in our lives? When will we humble ourselves and pray and seek His face and turn from our wicked ways? When will we command the power to fill our churches? If we have the power but no relationship with the Lord, the church will become man centered. If we have the relationship but no power, we will be too heavenly minded and lives will not be transformed. Jesus walked in oneness with the Father and He walked as a King with heavenly power and authority. When we, too, walk in both anointings simultaneously, there will be a CEASELESS FLOW OF OIL!!

Chapter 7: Understanding the Kingly

(The Kingly Inheritance)

One of the things that hold believers back from true, miraculous ministry is that they do not know the inheritance or the resources that were given to them by the Lord. If we ever lay hold of our inheritance by faith, signs, wonders and miracles will begin to break out as never before in order to touch and transform the lives of those God has called us to minister to. There are a few stories I will mention in this chapter in order to help us understand what our inheritance is and how to activate our inheritance by faith so we can see those miracles on a regular basis. When I began to receive my kingly inheritance, my ministry took a major turn toward the miraculous, and so will yours!!

1 Samuel 18:1-5 is a familiar story about Jonathan and David. We need to look at this story from a different perspective, however, as it is really a story that is a spiritual allegory. It reads:

"WHEN DAVID had finished speaking to Saul, the soul of Jonathan was knit with the soul of David, and Jonathan loved him as his own life. Saul took David that day and would not let him return to his father's house. Then Jonathan made a covenant with David, because he loved him as his own life. And Jonathan stripped himself of the robe that was on him and gave it to David, and his armor,

even his sword, his bow, and his girdle. And David went out wherever Saul sent him, and he prospered and behaved himself wisely; and Saul set him over the men of war. And it was satisfactory both to the people and to Saul's servants." (1 Samuel 18:1-5 AMP)

Let's go through this story line by line and precept upon precept so we can find out our kingly inheritance. Let's find the truths that are going to allow us to walk in the miraculous! Let's begin by understanding that there are three people mentioned in this passage: a Father, a Son, and a person outside of the family. Since this is an allegory, we can tell that they represent the Heavenly Father, Jesus the Son, and a lost unbeliever. In this passage we see the fact that the unbeliever, David, was so loved that Jonathan (Jesus) desired to become one with him, which represents salvation. At the point of salvation, the Father took the new believer, the new adopted son, into His own family, and would not allow David to return to his own house ever again. What a glorious picture of salvation! The Father and Son love us so much that we become one with the Son and are adopted into the household or family of the Heavenly Father Himself!! To top that off, He will never leave us nor forsake us, He will not let us go. We are His forever, we become a part of the household of faith.

Those truths of the allegory are very familiar to us and very dear and precious to us. Yet, that is all many Christians understand about their salvation. The next part is key and we must understand how deeply profound our inheritance is. It says that the Son came into a love covenant with him, making an unbreakable agreement with David. What agreement did He make that would change the course of David's life? Jonathan literally gave David His kingly inheritance. Jonathan was heir to the throne of His Father but chose to give away all the rights to the throne to David! This is an absolutely stunning event for that day and time. It is as if Prince Charles, heir to the throne of the kingdom of Great Britain, gave up all rights to the throne to some person off the street, totally losing all his rights to that kingly inheritance! This is exactly what Jesus has done for us (see also Romans 8:17). He was the Father's only Son and He gave up all rights to be King here on earth by giving us the kingship, giving us all authority and dominion on earth!! What was that inheritance? Jonathan first stripped himself of the royal robes he was wearing and placed them on David. This was symbolic of saying that he was literally stripping away his own inheritance as king and giving it to David!! That was not all David received, though, upon his entrance into the Kingdom or family of God. Jonathan then proceeded to give David his armor beginning with his sword. The sword represents power and anointing. We get all the same anointing and power that Jesus had when He walked on earth. Jesus gives us this power as our inheritance! He also gives us His bow. The bow was very important because the stronger the bow, the more powerful the arrows were launched to defeat the enemy. The bow represents victory over the enemy. If we only truly believed that we *always* are led in triumph, that we *always* win, that we are *always* more than conquerors because that is our inheritance!! If we lived our Christian lives from a position of victory, how much more powerful and effective and miraculous would we be? Jonathan also gave David his girdle. The girdle helped hold all of the king's armor and weapons in place. This symbolizes the New Testament truth that we are to "put on" various promises of Scripture as our portion. We are to put on the new man, put on the armor of Light, put on the Lord Jesus Christ, put on love, put on the full armor of God, put on grace, put on Jesus' yoke, put on my anointings and mantles, put on joy inexpressible and full of glory, etc. I have learned to daily put on these weapons and resources and each time I do it by faith I sense strongly in the Spirit that those weapons are activated and I know each one is available as I go out and about to minister. The miracles in my ministry began to greatly increase as I understood this part of my kingly inheritance!

The next part of the story explains that from that moment David became an extremely effective and successful soldier, winning miraculous victories and winning favor with those around him. THIS is our inheritance! We are kings, set apart with power and anointing to attack the forces of darkness and rescue the perishing! If we would get hold of the fact that EVERY believer is handed these gifts by Jesus Himself it will change our lives and ministries. We are now kings anointed and set apart for victories great and small.

Another story that shows us our kingly inheritance is found in Esther 5. That is the story of how Esther went before the king and found favor with the king. We know that this story is an allegory as well because it involves a king and his bride! How many times have we went before the King as his bride afraid at how He would respond to us, especially when the Law says we deserve to die! Praise God we are no longer under the Law, we are under grace, and sure enough Esther found grace or favor with the King and made her request. Before she made the request, however, the King made an incredible statement. He said to her (v. 5) that she could ask whatever she wished and it would be granted to her up to half the Kingdom!! What that statement meant was that the King was treating her as a joint heir of His kingdom! We, the bride, are joint heirs with the bridegroom and can boldly come to the throne of grace and ask for whatever we wish and it will be granted!! Imagine what the King had to offer and every bit of it was made available to the bride who was bold enough to come into His presence, find favor, and make her request known to the King! This is our inheritance! We are joint heirs with Jesus and ALL of the Kingdom has been made available to us! Every resource of heaven is available to lay hold of. It is important to note that Esther did not have selfish motives in her request, she was asking ultimately for the Kingdom of God, the Jews, be protected and blessed. She came to the King seeking first the Kingdom. She could have asked for riches and it would have been granted to her, but there was a much greater need, the Jews were in danger. If we would understand that our inheritance is to ask for any and every resource in order to extend God's Kingdom, we would humbly ask for every resource we could use to honor and glory the King and His Kingdom as well as to reach those outside the Kingdom and to grow and help those inside the Kingdom.

One more quick story, the story of the Prodigal Son. When he returned to the Father, he was showered with gifts, an inheritance he did not deserve.

"But the father said to his servants, Bring forth the best robe, and put it on him; and put a ring on his hand, and shoes on his feet: And bring hither the fatted calf, and kill it; and let us eat, and be merry: For this my son was dead, and is alive again; he was lost, and is found. And they began to be merry." Luke 15: 22-24.

First the son was given a new robe, again symbolizing his royalty. The son was then given a ring which symbolized that the son now had the same authority as the father. Shoes on his feet represented legal rights in the gates as shoes were used to seal the deal in legal affairs of the community, so the son was now the official legal representative or ambassador of the King. If all that wasn't enough, the son then was given not just provision, but the abundance worthy of a king, the fatted calf. Can you receive by faith your kingly inheritance? Can you believe the King has given you authority, dominion, power, joint heirship in the Kingdom, legal ambassadorship, miracle power, prosperity, etc.? If you can believe it, receive them by faith daily, and you will begin walking with the resources, the inheritance of a king, the very inheritance that Jesus deserved and walked in but passed on to you and me!!

Chapter 8: Understanding the Kingly

(The Gospel of the Kingdom)

Jesus taught a bunch on the Kingdom of God and the Kingdom of heaven. What is the difference? I believe that the Kingdom of God is the rule and reign of God that every person that has ever lived must choose to enter or become a citizen of, or reject in favor of the kingdom of darkness. The Kingdom of Heaven is the community of believers that are a part of the Kingdom of God and it describes their environment and atmosphere as a member of that culture. It would be like a person changing citizenship from Haiti to the United States and experiencing the vast difference in politics, education, prosperity, art, safety, blessings, and opportunities. When we choose to submit to the rule and reign of Jesus, we become citizens of heaven with all of heavens blessings available to us! We are actually to call down heaven to earth (see the Lord's Prayer)! We should exemplify and manifest the riches of heaven to the citizens of darkness in order to show them the glory and greatness of our King! This is why the Gospel of the Kingdom will be preached to every person before Jesus returns. They must know the while Gospel, not just the Gospel of salvation. Only then is true justice served. Every person must be given the opportunity to accept the rule and reign of Jesus and fully know the benefits of repentance or of turning from darkness to light. The Gospel of the Kingdom is GOOD NEWS! It could not truly be good news unless we were convicted of our sin (the bad news) first. But then we must not only witness to forgiveness of sin, but also to every heavenly blessing!

In order to enter the Kingdom of God one must be convicted of their sin and repent and believe the good news! If that person would believe in their heart that Jesus died for them and would confess with their mouth Jesus is Lord, that person will be saved! Saved from what? All of the works of the enemy! All of the schemes of the enemy! All that the enemy throws at us is now defeated and he can inn no wise touch us! We are rescued from enemy territory and put in a safe place. Yes, the enemy will never quit trying to get us to wander back into his kingdom and many times we will which opens the door to his destructive tactics again, but a citizen of heaven needs only to confess and repent to be put back in right standing in the Kingdom of heaven and again enjoy the full benefits thereof! The ceaseless flow of oil is a benefit of the Kingdom of God! As we mature in our relationship with Jesus (the priestly) and as we walk in the Kingdom of God (kingly), we will see the oil poured out powerfully and consistently.

How does the Kingdom of God and the Kingdom of heaven operate? By faith! Faith is the currency of the Kingdom. When we enter into the Kingdom there are many precious promises that are all yes and amen in Christ. Those promises are activated and manifested by faith. The way we used to think and the things we used to trust in are shaken out of us (whatever can be shaken will be shaken so that all that remains will be the Kingdom of Heaven). In the Kingdom of heaven are minds are renewed, we make choices about living in the world but not of the world, we trust God, not credit cards, insurance companies, doctors, or Presidents. We trust in the King of the Kingdom period. He will not allow us to trust in anything but Him, that would be trusting in idols or false gods. That does not mean we will never own a credit card or see a doctor or have an insurance payment, but the Kingdom of God is not dependent on any of those things that the world system depends on. When we choose to submit to the King of Kings and the Lord of Lords, we trust Him not only to save us from our sin but to take care of our every need. He is not only a King, He is also a Father. He is Provider, Protector, Sustainer, Revelator, Governor, and etc. He is our all in all. In order to see the ceaseless flow of oil we must get out of the world system and enter into the Kingdom of God system or the Kingdom of Heaven. He will meet our needs in miraculous and heavenly ways that will amaze us. No eye has seen nor ear heard nor mind imagined all that awaits His children and His citizens!

Let's be more practical. This is what a day in the Kingdom may look like. One wakes up and resubmits every part of their life to the King, to His rule and reign. That person gives up his agenda for the day, his common sense, his ways, and receives God's wisdom, His mind, His agenda, His perfect will for the day. Then the King provides that person with everything he needs for life that day. The Lord may have to provide healing, finances, food, favor, love, grace, etc. He also releases everything the person needs for godliness. He gives holiness, a way of escape from temptation, anointings, divine opportunities, revelation, deliverance, etc. Then that person is fully equipped with God's presence, power, glory, provision, protection, and everything else to see that His citizens live a blessed life and that others enter the Kingdom through their loving witness.

Sounds so wonderful right? Then why do we see so little manifestation of Kingdom living? It is because we still are walking with one foot in the world and one foot in the Kingdom of God. We still trust in our credit score, we still trust in our jobs to provide for our needs, we go to the doctor before we ever ask Jehovah Rapha for our healing, we trust more in what we see then what we do not see, we walk by sight instead of by faith. Going through the tabernacle pattern of discipleship and spiritual growth and learning to live as a Kingdom citizen with a kingly anointing sets us up to walk in all the good and perfect gifts the Lord has for us, including the ceaseless flow.

It may take going through the Kingdom school of growth to learn how to live in the Kingdom, but that education will be well worth it. We have got to get out of our minds and into His mind, His understanding and do things His way. His ways are much higher than our ways and really do make us free. Let us get into the Kingdom of God and live like citizens of heaven! Let's study and meditate on every promise and then believe them without doubting and watch them manifest until there is a ceaseless flow! Lord, do this work quickly in us as right now we choose Your Kingdom! We submit to You as the King of all creation and the King of all the universe. We renounce the world, its ways, its economy, its bondages, and its leader, the devil. We choose this day to walk by faith and we surrender all of our life to you, we choose to be delivered from all evil, to receive the Kingdom empowerment of the Holy Spirit, to receive a Spirit of wisdom and revelation in the knowledge of Jesus, to intensely seek You through prayer and worship, and to believe every promise is yes and amen in Christ in the Holy of Holies. We also choose to get our lives under Kingdom government, to walk as kings submitted to the King of kings, to be in divine order, to take dominion again, and to be royal ambassadors for Your glory! We believe, Father, that the ceaseless flow of oil is then released unto us!!!

Chapter 9: What to do with the Oil

Zechariah promises us that there are two trees that are pouring out a ceaseless flow of oil, of grace, of power, of anointing, of favor, of finances, of salvations, of miracles, of blessing, of all His promises. When we realize that our own self effort, programs, and works have gotten us practically nowhere in two thousand years (the world does not seem to be getting better although we were commissioned to make disciples of all nations, nor does the church seem to be getting better), we hunger like Zechariah did to understand what the two trees represented. The revelation that the two trees represent the priestly and the kingly bears witness to Jesus Himself who is our King and our Priest. As one begins to grow through the journey of the tabernacle pattern of spiritual growth and as one understands their destiny and calling as a king and begin walking it out, he will begin to see trickles of oil. The more one walks out these two anointings, the more the flow becomes a gusher, a ceaseless flow that takes us from grace to mega grace, glory to new realms of glory, and from former rain to latter rain.

When will the world be impacted by the church? When the ceaseless flow becomes a reality. Let's finish with two last stories from the Old Testament about a ceaseless flow that symbolizes what the Lord wants to do in these last days. The first is found in 2 Kings 4:1-6.

"Now the wife of a son of the prophets cried to Elisha, Your servant my husband is dead, and you know that your servant feared the Lord. But the creditor has come to take my two sons to be his slaves. Elisha said to her, What shall I do for you? Tell me, what have you [of sale value] in the house? She said, Your handmaid has nothing in the house except a jar of oil. Then he said, Go around and borrow vessels from all your neighbors, empty vessels—and not a few. And when you come in, shut the door upon you and your sons. Then pour out [the oil you have] into all those vessels, setting aside each one when it is full. So she went from him and shut the door upon herself and her sons, who brought to her the vessels as she poured the oil. When the vessels were all full, she said to her son, Bring me another vessel. And he said to her, There is not a one left. Then the oil stopped multiplying."

Just as the widow had a little oil, we all have a little oil, a little power, a little grace, a little love, and a little anointing of the Holy Spirit manifesting in our lives. Unfortunately, we do not have enough flow of oil to see breakthrough significant enough to get the world's attention off of themselves and on to Jesus. We have become the tail instead of being the head. The Body of Christ is in a place of desperation. But in this season the Lord is sending apostles, prophets, evangelists, pastors, and teachers to tell us that the way to reach the world is to take the little oil we have and turn it into a ceaseless flow. The way to do that is what this book is all about. As the oil begins to flow, we know it is time for the Lord to send us out to find empty vessels, the hurting people of our neighborhoods, communities, cities, and nations. Then we can pour out the oil into their lives until they are full and ready to be poured out to others. We are way past the day of seeing them saved and left sitting in a pew. As we pour out the oil that the Lord is pouring into us, we will see the oil never run out. It will be a ceaseless flow. It will only run out if we quit finding empty, hurting vessels that need the miraculous, powerful, wonderful, loving, life-changing touch of God.

As we become kings and priests and the oil begins to flow, all we need to do is to then go and make disciples of all nations. The Lord will lead us directly to these people just as He led Philip to the Ethiopian eunuch. You will encounter many divine appointments, and the saints of the world will literally turn the world upside down and right side up!

The second is found in Ezekiel 47:1-10:

"Then he brought me back to the door of the house; and behold, water was flowing from under the threshold of the house toward the east, for the house faced east. And the water was flowing down from under, from the right side of the house, from south of the altar. He brought me out by way of the north gate and led me around on the outside to the outer gate by way of the gate that faces east. And behold, water was trickling from the south side. When the man went out toward the east with a line in his hand, he measured a thousand cubits, and he led me through the water, water reaching the ankles. Again he measured a thousand and led me through the water, water reaching the knees. Again he measured a thousand and led me through the water, water reaching the loins. Again he measured a thousand; and it was a river that I could not ford, for the water had risen, enough water to swim in, a river that could not be forded. He said to me, "Son of man, have you seen this?" Then he brought me back to the bank of the river. Now when I had returned, behold, on the bank of the river there were very many trees on the one side and on the other. Then he said to me, "These waters go out toward the eastern region and go down into the Arabah; then they go toward the sea, being made to flow into the sea, and the waters of the sea become fresh . "It will come about that every living creature which swarms in every place where the river goes, will live. And there will be very many fish, for these waters go there and the others become fresh; so everything will live where the river goes. "And it will come about that fishermen will stand beside it; from

Engedi to Eneglaim there will be a place for the spreading of nets. Their fish will be according to their kinds, like the fish of the Great Sea, very many."

This story talks about a flow of water that starts in the Temple and flows out of the church toward the world. As the water flows it is a trickle but it is important for us in this study to understand where the flow began. It began in the Holy of Holies. As the water begins to trickle out, it gets deeper and deeper and more ceaseless as it flows away from the church and out toward the lost fish. When the flow of the Holy Spirit hits the sea where the fish are, the passage says that wherever the river goes, the creatures will live! Oh how the world needs the flow leading to His Life!! Lord we beg of You to release this flow where the spiritually dead become alive as we spread out our evangelistic nets! This ceaseless flow is real, God desires it more than we do, and He will move upon those who surrender all and risk all to enter the Holy of Holies. The flow will begin and as we go out, the flow becomes ceaseless! Let's enter the Presence of the Lord and begin to carry that Presence out of our church services and into the world. We will see the Life-giving flow touch the world!

The world needs this ceaseless flow of oil. Hurting people demand it. The heart and love of God demands it. We need to demand it. Deep darkness is covering the people. Let the glory of the Lord begin to arise around you and shine upon you until kings come to your light! May you, your family, your church, your community, and your nation be swept up in the ceaseless flow of God's presence, love, grace, and power!

Chapter 10: Digging New Wells

This journey to experience revival has been the greatest journey of my life, the most exciting and fun days of ministry I have ever known, yet it has resulted in some of the hardest lessons and obstacles from the enemy I have ever experienced. It will always be this way for forerunners, for those breaking out new wineskins, for those digging new wells. This is because the enemy wants to stop the unceasing flow of oil and the last great revival in history more that anything else. The Lord was gracious in giving us understanding of this process through two passages about digging wells, one in Genesis 26, the other in Numbers 21.

Chapter 26 is a fascinating chapter because it typifies the church today. The chapter starts off by setting the picture of what time it was in the natural. It was a time of famine. Of course, we know that the Old Testament is a type and shadow of the New, and we can find many spiritual parallels to our lives as well. Just as it was a time of famine in Genesis 26, the Body of Christ in many places around the world is in a time of spiritual famine. Isaac starts to move his family away from the famine to go to Egypt, a place of abundance. As we know, however, Egypt is a type of the world and the world system. The Lord speaks to Isaac and tells him not to go to Egypt, not to go to the world to see his needs met, he was to dwell where Abraham had dwelt, the place of covenant, the place of abundance, the place where he could stand upon the shoulders of his father. So Isaac dwells there and we see in v. 18 that Isaac's servants began to redig the wells that Abraham had dug but that the enemy had filled in. The church must realize that the enemy wants us to neglect the truths our forefathers have given to the Body of Christ over the years. He wants them to stay buried. He wants us to forget about Jonathan Edwards, John Wesley, Charles Finney, Azusa Street, Billy Graham, Smith Wigglesworth, Oral Roberts, the Word of faith movement, the prophetic movement, etc. We are not to neglect those truths, we are to build upon them. Did they have it all right back then? No. Neither will we have it all right today, but we must mine the gold of the past in order to find new veins today. So, Isaac's servants began to re-dig the old wells of Abraham. This is an exciting time for the church. We re-dug the old wells because many of our people had never experienced those truths. Some had even been told not to follow those movements and so they never understood them or checked them against Scripture to see if there was any value in them. The more we dug the old, the more we understood, the more we tasted of treasures old and new, the more excitement built.

Notice that Isaac's servants did not stop digging there. They kept on digging. We must never be content to live off the old. God is always doing a new thing and we need to stay on the edge of what He is doing. We need to keep digging new wells. Unfortunately, the new wells that Isaac dug were named Strife and Contention. Understand that Jesus said we are to count the cost as His disciples. Understand now that if you begin digging new wells as a church you will face strife and contention. The battle may be short, it may be long, but it will be there. You will experience persecution, times of frustration, and many difficult days. Mark 4, the parable of the sower, tells us that every Word of the Lord we receive will be tested by the enemy and he will try to steal the Word. The enemy knows that if the Word is stolen or choked out or scorched, it will never bear 100-fold fruit. So during the days of teaching these truths to the people, much contention arose. We battled several principalities that tried to stop this truth from bearing fruit. We battled the religious spirit, the jezebel spirit, the Absalom spirit, the antichrist spirit, and the spirit of fear as well as others. You, too, will have to dig wells of contention and strife before you dig the well of fruitfulness.

The good news of this story is that the servants kept digging. There are many wonderful promises to the Christian that overcomes and perseveres. The next well that they dug was the well of fruitfulness! The well after that was Beersheba, the well of covenant! That is the place where the Lord showed up and Isaac ultimately pitched his tent. That is where I want to pitch my tent, the place of His presence! All who dig face struggles, but the end result is worth it. There are no shortcuts. The churches that take the shortcuts will never experience the Holy of Holies, the place of His Covenant Presence. Shortcuts will get us what we have always got, old wells. Today many churches are pitching their tent at the old wells. Many are reaching the lost and are big evangelistic centers. Praise God for them. Many churches are experiencing signs and wonders and healings. Hallelujah! But how many churches are transforming their cities with the Presence of God as they did in the New Testament? It is the Presence of God alone that transforms people, not programs left over the 50's, 80's, last year, or even from the last powerful move of the Spirit. We must keep digging these new wells.

How do we dig these wells? Numbers 21:16-20 shows us how to dig spiritual wells:

"From there they continued to Beer, that is the well where the LORD said to Moses, 'Assemble the people, that I may give them water.' Then Israel sang this song: 'Spring up, O well! Sing to it! The well, which the leaders sank, Which the nobles of the people dug, With the scepter and with their staffs.' And from the wilderness they continued to Mattanah, and from Mattanah to Nahaliel, and from Nahaliel to Bamoth, and from Bamoth to the valley that is in the land of Moab, at the top of Pisgah which overlooks the wasteland." (Numbers 21:16-20 NASB)

Notice first the four principles of digging. First, they sang to the well. Obviously, this is referring to the Holy Spirit. So they worshipped. There will be no wells dug without worship. Worship is the strategy for every new move of God. Without worship, man has a tendency to think it is his own hand that brings revival. Our digging is only meaningful when we dig His way in His location while praising Him! Yes, we have a part called faithfulness. But the wells are His and He must be worshipped! No new well will be worth anything if the Presence of God is not at the forefront. The wells we want to dig must be about Him. The well will not attract Him if worship is not involved. He is attracted to where He is being praised and adored.

Secondly, we notice that wells are dug with unity. The passage says that Moses was to gather the people together. Also, the word translated "nobles" in this passage can be translated "all who are willing." The Body of Christ is yet to see the power of a group of people absolutely committed to one another and to the call of God and are absolutely willing to dig no matter the cost! This key element is discussed in another later chapter but suffice it to say now that according to John 21:17 there will be no outbreak of the glory of God without unity. There will be no evangelism and there will be no anointing of life according to Psalm 133. Genesis 11:6 tells us that at the Tower of Babel the Lord recognized the power of their unity in a negative direction so He only had to destroy the unity to stop the tower from prospering. The enemy knows this too and has been very good, unfortunately, at stopping the unity among believers today. When unity comes, so does the new well of God's presence and glory!

Thirdly, the wells were dug by the leaders (princes or governors) with their scepter or their authority or their decrees. This passage refers to the kingly role we will discuss later. When we walk in our authority, the well will be dug. We are to make authoritative decrees and declarations according to what the Lord has already said in His Word or through rhema words. Isn't it interesting that ancient peoples used to search for wells with "divining rods"? Upon the authority of their witchcraft, they would dig a well. Upon our authority of the Word of God we will know when to dig, where to dig, what to dig, how to dig, and when to dig. When we get a word from the Lord we can stand on it, believe it, confess it, and act upon it with full assurance that the word will come to pass. Digging is hard work, so is making faith declarations. But without standing by faith, God will not move because He only responds to faith, according to our faith it will be done unto us. They even sang with authority, "Spring up O well!"

Lastly, the nobles or all who were willing dug with their staffs. A staff represents love. Oh, yes, that forgotten essential called love. Love compels us, covers others, drives our passion for God and for the lost, love never fails, love results in the world being reached, love is the first and second greatest commandments. When we put worship, unity, authority, and love together, we will see old wells re-dug and new wells opened and flowing.

Before we move on, let's take a quick look at the results of digging the wells in this passage. We know that the wells symbolize living waters, moves of the Holy Spirit. By looking at the names of the locations the Israelites moved to after they dug the wells, we will see the progression of what will happen in the Body of Christ when the wells of the Holy Spirit are dug. After they dug the wells the passage tells us that they moved away from the wilderness! How many believers are still in the wilderness! Oh to move out of the desert place spiritually. We will only move out as we dig these old and new wells. From the wilderness, they moved to Mattanah which comes from the root word meaning gifts. Let us move from the wilderness to the gifts of the Holy Spirit! Then they moved on to Nahaliel, which means God of the mighty river. Do we need a mighty move of the river of God? Yes, desperately! From the wilderness they went to the gifts, from the gifts they went to the mighty river or move of God, then they went to Bamoth which is the plural of the Hebrew word meaning the high place! The high places of the world, flesh, and the devil will be destroyed and God will be restored to the high place as will His children. Dominion restored! Authority restored! Victory, being more than conquerors,

God doing exceedingly abundantly more than we can ask or imagine! Is this not what we have been praying for and crying out for? Then dig! If that is not enough to make us dig, they went one more place, Pisgah, the cleft of the rock. The end result of the digging was the Rock of Jesus, Christlikeness, His fullness! This was the place that overlooked the Promised Land which was then achievable! Praise the Lord for His goodness and His plan to bless us and make us a Kingdom of priests and overcomers and world changers! Get out your shovels of worship, unity, authority and love! Let's begin today!

Chapter 11: The Key to Sustained Revival in America!

On my first trip to Pakistan, I was expecting the Lord to do great things. Why else would He send me to a place no one else seemed to want to go? But I had said yes to the Lord many years ago, so going was not an option. I arrived there with a couple friends and we began to minister right away. It was late when we arrived and we prayed for the pastors that had driven many miles to meet us at the airport. Nothing really spectacular happened but it was nice to meet them. The next night we ministered in a small village. We shared some testimonies and a few short messages and then prayed for the people. Again, nothing really supernatural was happening. So that night when I went to bed I couldn't sleep. All I could think was that the Lord did not send me all the way to Pakistan for little to no results. So I paced my bedroom floor for a few hours praying and asking the Lord what the problem was. Little did I know, He was about to reveal to me something that would change me, Pakistan, and America!!

As I paced the bedroom floor the Lord gave me a vision. I saw women from the village gathered in one of the ladies' homes and they were decreeing something over their village. I saw children running around the house but the ladies were focused on their decrees and they were decreeing very intensely. I didn't even know what they were decreeing but I could tell they were very passionate and focused. Then the Spirit spoke to me and said, "That is the key to revival in Pakistan." That was all I saw in the spirit. I somehow felt that He had answered my prayer so I went to bed. I did not even hardly remember the vision all that day because I was focused on preaching that evening at the service. I was all prepared as the service began but as I got up to speak the Spirit told me not to preach my message but to share the vision He had given me in the middle of the night as I was praying.

So, I began to share the vision with the congregation. As I was sharing the vision, the Lord was telling me what they were decreeing! I was sharing and listening to the Lord at the same time. The Spirit told me that they were decreeing Galatians 3:13-14 which says, *"Christ redeemed us from the curse of the law by becoming a curse for us—for it is written, "Cursed is everyone who is hanged on a tree"— so that in Christ Jesus the blessing of Abraham might come to the Gentiles, so that we might receive the promised Spirit through faith.""* I knew that if they would just join hands with two or three others in agreement and if they began to intensely decree that every curse was broken off their village by the blood of Jesus and that the blessing of Abraham was being released to them (blessing of Abraham is first a blessing of faith) and if they decreed that an outpouring of the Spirit was being released, then revival would break out in Pakistan!! So, I shared the vision and then told them that the decree was Galatians 3:13-14 and what that meant and then the Lord spoke to me and told me to have them do that right then. I then told them to begin to get in groups of two to three people, grab their hands and with agreement of faith call in Galatians 3:13-14. To my surprise they had really no idea of what I was trying to say. It literally took me about 15 minutes to explain what it meant to hold someone's had and agree in prayer with them. They did not get it until I gathered some people on the platform to show them what that would look like. They finally understood so they began to grab people's hands. I can't say there were many groups of two or three holding hands in a circle, there were some groups like that but for the most part there were large groups in a line holding hands. But all that mattered was their agreement with and declaration of Galatians 3:13-14. So, I asked them to begin decreeing and did they ever!! The same passion and intensity I had seen in the vision began happening before my eyes as they began shouting and declaring those verses. Then I will never forget what happened next, the Holy Spirit fell in that room unlike I have ever experienced! The presence of God came suddenly and immersed us to the point I did not know what to do. I was almost afraid to move or say anything because I did not want to get in the way of what He was doing. So, I just stood there for a few moments trying to figure out what in the world just happened and what we should do next. So eventually I turned around and looked at the ministry team on the platform and asked what they thought we should do. Someone then said that we should go out into the congregation and begin praying for the people. So we did. The next thing I knew we started seeing miracles and healings that I had never seen anywhere in my ministry but had only longed for. Deaf mutes were hearing and speaking, all sorts of healings and deliverances broke out! A group of youth girls called me over and began prophesying over my life very accurately, some just fell out in the Spirit without being touched. About 80% of the congregation experienced a healing!

Every kind of miracle broke out in Pakistan that day and much more has happened since! Blind eyes opening, cancer healed, tumors melting off bodies, TB healed, hepatitis healed, paralysis healed, people getting out of wheelchairs, barren women healed and began conceiving and having babies, financial miracles began being released, major deliverances from Muslim spirits, etc. became normal! I just received a report of a one-month old baby being resurrected from the dead there. Few nights later was when we saw the babies praying for the sick and seeing them healed. It is not unusual now to see 100% healings in meetings. We have seen thousands upon thousands of people instantly saved and healed. We often say 80% healings is now a bad day there! Impartations have been released so the people there are walking in crazy miracles! Young and old have been transformed and revival is spreading. The key to revival was two or three believers coming into agreement and declaring Galatians 3:13-14.

As I sat on the plane riding home from Pakistan around 2am, the Lord got my attention and told me that He had something to say to me. So I put down all my electronics and got quiet and began listening. The Lord spoke so clearly to me right then and He said, "The key to revival I showed you for Pakistan is also the key to revival for America." I was stunned but I had just seen it work supernaturally and all of a sudden, I got extremely excited about what the Lord was going to do in America. When I got home from Pakistan I immediately began sharing about what I had seen and heard in Pakistan but that the key to revival there was also being released in America. We began to form "ecclesias" of two or three and intensely calling in Galatians 3:13-14. We are now seeing some similar things here that we saw there! The fire of God is falling so powerfully here that we have never experienced anything like it.

So what does all that mean? It means that it is time for the Church to be the Church again as defined in the Bible, not in practice in American churches. The word church in our English translations is the word ecclesia in Greek. That word never meant a building with a preacher and pulpit and choir robes and announcements. In biblical days anyone hearing the word ecclesia would have known that it meant a gathering of people together for the purpose of making governmental decisions. Ecclesia is even used in the New Testament in that way, see Acts 19:32, 39, 41. To original believers, they never saw the church as a building, they saw it as a governmental body. Jesus shows this to be the case in Matthew 16:16. He describes the ecclesia, the church, as those who have power and authority to bind and loose which were the governmental keys or the keys of the Kingdom. Later, in Matthew 18, Jesus elaborates the point after talking again about binding and loosing and says that whenever two or three gather together in His name, His presence would manifest and they could decree things and it would absolutely be done for them! The Greek word there for pray also means to require. When Jesus taught us to pray He literally said in Greek, "I command you to pray in this manner, Our

Father in heaven, we command your name to be hallowed, we command your Kingdom to come and your will to be done on earth as it is in heaven, we command daily bread to come, we command deliverance from evil and we command forgiving of debts." These were governmental decrees that Jesus told us were not optional!! So when He showed me this in Pakistan and we did it, He HAD to loose deliverances, faith, and an outpouring of the Spirit and He did!!

Today the church must get back to the truth of what the true church or ecclesia is. It is two or three gathered in His name to govern or co-rule and co-reign with Him. We gather, He shows up, He speaks, we believe it in our heart and then we confess it and decree it governmentally with authority and then it comes to pass! What would happen if the church became the Church again?! I can tell you that revival would break out because we have experienced it on a regular basis! It is the key to revival in America and everywhere, being the original Church again! This matched the understanding of Zechariah chapter 4 of how to see a ceaseless flow of oil, to be kings and priests. There are many things we hear from the Lord and decree as an ecclesia, not just Galatians 3:13-14. But that verse is a key verse for these last days.

One last thing. Jesus told Peter in Matthew 16 when talking about the governmental role of the church of binding and loosing that the gates of hell will not prevail against the ecclesia. If the gates of hell are prevailing against our families, ministries, and regions, it is because we are not being the ecclesia! When we began to be governmental in our ministry, revival broke out and it has been sustained. If we meet in a building, sing some awesome anointed songs, preach an anointed message, but never do anything governmental, we have not been the church! We have seen here in America God do amazing things, resurrections from the dead, blind eyes open, cripples walk, cancers healed, you name it. In Pakistan we have seen people that were walking past the meeting get saved and healed. We have seen people carried in almost dying get healed just in the presence because we have already declared governmentally what He told us to decree over that meeting. We now have learned and continue to learn more about how to be the church, the government of God, the kings and priests that are chosen by God to declare His praises and to reach the uttermost parts of the world. Will you join us? A ceaseless flow of Holy Spirit oil will begin to flow to you and will change your life, your family, your ministry, and your region forever for the glory of Jesus!!!

57502730R00063

Made in the USA
Columbia, SC
12 May 2019